Improving C Blood Lead Level Screening, Reporting, and Surveillance in Allegheny County, Pennsylvania

Donna Keyser, Ray Firth, Amy Richardson,
Maria Zeglen Townsend

Prepared for Healthy Home Resources

 HEALTH

The research described in the report was conducted in RAND Health, a division of the RAND Corporation, for Healthy Home Resources.

Library of Congress Cataloging-in-Publication Data

Improving childhood blood lead level screening, reporting, and surveillance in Allegheny county, Pennsylvania / Donna Keyser ... [et al.].
    p. ; cm.
    "MG-423."
    Includes bibliographical references.
    ISBN 0-8330-3945-8 (pbk. : alk. paper)
    1. Lead poisoning in children—Pennsylvania—Allegheny County—Prevention—
Statistics. 2. Medical screening—Pennsylvania—Allegheny County.
I. Keyser, Donna. II. Rand Corporation.
    [DNLM: 1. Lead Poisoning—blood—Pennsylvania. 2. Lead Poisoning—
epidemiology—Pennsylvania. 3. Child—Pennsylvania. 4. Infant—Pennsylvania.
5. Mass Screening—Pennsylvania. 6. Program Evaluation—Pennsylvania. 7. Safety
Management—Pennsylvania. QV 292 I34 2006]

RA1251.L4I47 2006
615.9'256880974885—dc22

                                                  2006010689

The RAND Corporation is a nonprofit research organization providing objective analysis and effective solutions that address the challenges facing the public and private sectors around the world. RAND's publications do not necessarily reflect the opinions of its research clients and sponsors.

RAND® is a registered trademark.

A profile of RAND Health, abstracts of its publications, and ordering information can be found on the RAND Health home page at www.rand.org/health.

Published 2006 by the RAND Corporation
1776 Main Street, P.O. Box 2138, Santa Monica, CA 90407-2138
1200 South Hayes Street, Arlington, VA 22202-5050
4570 Fifth Avenue, Suite 600, Pittsburgh, PA 15213-2612
RAND URL: http://www.rand.org/
To order RAND documents or to obtain additional information, contact
Distribution Services: Telephone: (310) 451-7002;
Fax: (310) 451-6915; Email: order@rand.org

Preface

One of the key goals of current U.S. public health policy is the elimination of childhood lead poisoning. To further this goal at the community level, Healthy Home Resources commissioned the RAND Corporation and the University of Pittsburgh Office of Child Development to examine the current status of childhood blood lead level screening, reporting, and surveillance in Allegheny County, Pennsylvania, and to offer recommendations for improving these processes. The findings and recommendations presented in this report are the result of a background study of the relevant literature; a review of existing blood lead level reporting and surveillance databases for Pennsylvania and Allegheny County; and interviews and focus groups with national, state, and local stakeholders. The recommendations were further enhanced and refined through discussions with an advisory group composed of state and local policymakers, health care and health plan providers, parents, and representatives from Healthy Home Resources.

This report is intended primarily for state and local policymakers, public health officials, health care and health plan providers, local government agencies, and parents interested in improving childhood blood lead level screening, reporting, and surveillance in Allegheny County. However, some of the recommendations may be useful to other states, counties, and local communities seeking to make similar improvements in their childhood blood lead level screening, reporting, and surveillance processes. This research was conducted in RAND Health, a division of the RAND Corporation. A profile of RAND Health, abstracts of its publications, and ordering information can be found at www.rand.org/health. Questions and comments about this report are welcome and should be addressed to the principal investigator:

Donna J. Keyser, Ph.D., MBA
Associate Director
RAND Corporation–University of Pittsburgh Health Institute
4570 Fifth Avenue, Suite 600
Pittsburgh, PA 15213-2665
(412) 683-2300 x4928
Email: Donna_Keyser@rand.org

Contents

Figures

Tables

Summary

Lead poisoning is a serious, preventable environmental health threat to young children in many communities throughout the United States (AAP, Committee on Environmental Health, 1998). One of the key goals for U.S. public health policy included in the U.S. Department of Health and Human Services (HHS) *Healthy People 2010* report is the elimination of elevated blood lead levels in children (see HHS, 2000). Achievement of this goal will require improvements in three general areas: (1) lead poisoning prevention; (2) screening, reporting, and surveillance of childhood blood lead levels; and (3) treatment of childhood lead poisoning. The focus of this report is on screening, reporting, and surveillance, which are critical, not only to the overall goal of eliminating lead poisoning, but to its prevention and treatment as well.

Fortunately, past efforts focused primarily on lead poisoning prevention have led to a decline in the number of children nationwide with elevated blood lead levels. Between 1999 and 2002, 1.6 percent of children one to five years old, or 310,000, had blood lead levels at or above the current recommended cutoff of 10 micrograms of lead per deciliter of blood (μg/dL), compared to 88.2 percent between 1976 and 1980 (CDC, 2005). Despite this significant reduction in the number of children nationally between the ages of one and five years who have elevated blood lead levels and the lower levels of blood lead observed, a number of issues continue to complicate effective eradication of this important public health problem.

First, the general perception that the problem of childhood lead poisoning has been resolved must be corrected. To place the rate of high lead levels (i.e., 1.6 percent of children nationwide) in context, the national prevalence rates for autism, childhood depression, and attention deficit hyperactivity disorder—other childhood health problems currently considered to be of critical concern—are 0.91 percent, 5 percent, and 3 to 5 percent, respectively (American Academy of Child and Adolescent Psychiatry, 2004a, 2004c, 2004b). Unlike these other conditions, however, the causes of childhood lead poisoning are known, and the condition is 100-percent preventable.

Second, recent national blood lead level data continue to show a clear racial disparity. Although the largest decrease in elevated blood lead levels (from 11.2 percent in 1991–1994 to 3.1 percent in 1999–2002) has been among non-Hispanic black children aged one to five years, this group of young children remains at greater risk for exposure to harmful lead levels than non-Hispanic white children (1.3 percent) and Mexican-American children (2.0 percent) in the same age range (CDC, 2005). The risk of elevated blood lead levels also remains higher for other subpopulations of young children, including children from low-income families and children who live in older homes (CDC, 1997).

Third, because most young children with elevated blood lead levels have no obvious symptoms at the time of exposure, the prevention, detection, assessment, and management of lead poisoning and associated risk factors rely entirely on the results of blood lead screening tests.

Fourth, the absence of obvious symptoms belies the negative impact that even low levels of blood lead (i.e., less than 10 µg/dL) can have on a young child's cognitive, intellectual, and neurodevelopmental outcomes, and the very serious implications that these outcomes have for broader issues of national concern, such as school readiness and educational achievement levels.

Fifth, although eliminating childhood lead poisoning remains a high priority on the national public health agenda, responsibility for ensuring that at-risk young children are screened for lead poisoning and that the results are reported to relevant authorities is often fragmented at the county level, hindering adequate prevention, surveillance, and treatment efforts. In Pennsylvania, for example, all blood lead screening results must be reported directly to the state's disease-surveillance system by health care providers or state-licensed laboratories. The Allegheny County Health Department (ACHD) is no longer the first recipient of this data. Its current responsibility is limited to case management for those children identified as having elevated blood lead levels based on data reported at the state level.

For all of these reasons, now more than ever, effective screening, reporting, and surveillance of childhood lead poisoning requires the concerted, proactive, and coordinated effort of state and local public health officials, health care and health plan providers, community agencies, and parents. Such efforts are particularly important in communities with high rates of reported elevated blood lead levels or with inadequate data on the prevalence of elevated blood lead levels, as well as in communities with older housing, which increases the risk of young children's exposure to harmful lead levels.

Pittsburgh ranks 28th on the Centers for Disease Control and Prevention (CDC) list of the 129 cities with the greatest number of children estimated to have elevated blood lead levels (PA DOH, 2005). The CDC and the American Academy of Pediatrics (AAP) recommend that communities with comparable blood lead levels institute universal, rather than targeted or selected, blood lead screening. Moreover, many children in Allegheny County belong to high-risk groups (i.e., they live in households that are below the poverty level or in census tracts where the median-year housing was built before 1950).

In light of the issues raised above, the RAND Corporation, in collaboration with the University of Pittsburgh Office of Child Development, was commissioned by Healthy Home Resources to do the following:

- Review the quality of existing data on blood lead screening, reporting, and surveillance for young children in Allegheny County, and, if feasible, to use this data for estimating (1) the prevalence of childhood lead poisoning in Allegheny County and (2) the number of young children in Allegheny County with blood lead levels of 10 µg/dL or greater who have not been screened.
- Identify key barriers to screening, reporting, and surveillance efforts in Allegheny County, and potential strategies for overcoming them.
- Develop a set of recommendations for improving screening, reporting, and surveillance in Allegheny County.

Existing Data on Childhood Blood Lead Screening, Reporting, and Surveillance in Allegheny County

Data on blood lead screening from three extant databases were examined: the National Health and Nutrition Examination Survey (NHANES), the Pennsylvania National Electronic Disease Surveillance System (PA-NEDSS), and the Pennsylvania Medicaid database. An analysis of each database with regard to data characteristics and data quality revealed the following:

- The NHANES sample selection process and overall study methodology ensure the reliability of its results for the nation as a whole. However, the ability to make predictions from this data regarding local prevalence rates is limited. At best, these data provide an *approximate* range of the number of children with elevated blood lead levels in Allegheny County.
- PA-NEDSS has significant potential for providing comprehensive, timely, and high-quality data. However, the lead component of PA-NEDSS currently has a number of limitations: a quality review process that has only recently been implemented, missing information, an inability to assess the completeness of reporting, and an inability to cross-reference the information with Medicaid data.
- Medicaid claims data indicate only that a lead screening was completed and a claim was submitted; they do not specify blood lead levels in children who were screened nor whether the blood lead levels were elevated. The Medicaid database does include the ages of all children enrolled in Medicaid and, if applicable, their physical health managed care organizations (MCOs) and primary care providers. Thus, the relevant MCO or Office of Medical Assistance Program (OMAP) can

determine which Medicaid children are missing a lead screening and follow up as needed to ensure that blood lead level screenings are conducted in compliance with Medicaid requirements.

Based on the available data, we compared Allegheny County's screening and prevalence rates for childhood lead poisoning with other regions that have comparable levels of risk for childhood lead poisoning. The range of all children screened for childhood lead poisoning varies from 15.3 percent in Erie County to 2 percent in both Lancaster and Chester Counties; Allegheny County ranks sixth, with 5.4 percent of young children screened. Allegheny County's screening rate for children enrolled in Medicaid is fifth among the 12 Pennsylvania counties. Prevalence rates of blood lead levels of 10 µg/dL or greater among children screened under the age of six years range from 5 percent in Chester County to 22 percent in Lancaster County. Allegheny County's prevalence rate of 5.9 percent ranks it fourth lowest among the 12 counties. In comparison, Rhode Island's screening rate is 87 percent, and the prevalence rate for lead poisoning in this state (which is approximately the same size as Allegheny County) has declined to below 4 percent in 2003 from more than 14 percent a decade ago.

Given the limitations of the data described above, it is impossible to know with certainty the extent of the childhood lead poisoning problem in Allegheny County. However, estimates based on the available data suggest that 987 children between the ages of one and five years and 1,771 children under the age of six years with Medicaid benefits who have not been screened are likely to have blood lead levels of 10 µg/dL or greater.

Screening for Childhood Lead Poisoning in Allegheny County

According to the 1998 Medicaid Manual, a lead screening test must be provided to all children 12 to 24 months old who are enrolled in Medicaid. A child between 36 and 72 months of age who has not received a prior blood lead screening test must be screened. No risk assessment is required. For all other children, the blood lead screening recommendations of the CDC or the Health Resources and Service Administration should be followed as appropriate and unless superseded by state or county recommendations. The Pennsylvania Department of Health (PA DOH) Lead Elimination Plan calls for universal screening of all children without a confirmed prior blood lead test at the ages of one and two years and of all children three to six years old (PA DOH, 2005). The ACHD endorses the PA DOH's call for universal screening of all children at the ages one and two years.

Although national surveys of pediatricians indicate that they know the Medicaid requirements and CDC recommendations for childhood lead screening, available data at the national, state, and local levels suggest that these guidelines are often not followed. A number of barriers currently work against adequate childhood lead screening in Allegheny County.

First, the dramatic reduction in extremely high blood lead levels in young children has reinforced the general perception that childhood lead poisoning is no longer a public health concern and that screening is not important for young children. Second, federal screening requirements and state and local screening recommendations notwithstanding, many health care providers may be following a policy of targeted screening, which adds several decision points to the determination that a child is at risk for lead poisoning. At each of these decision points, some at-risk children may not be identified and therefore not screened. Third, there are reported concerns about drawing blood from young children, the appropriateness of capillary samples, and the skills of the staff collecting the samples. Fourth, because many health care providers prefer to conduct lead screening tests through venous blood draws and do not have a readily available pediatric blood-drawer, many children are referred to off-site laboratories for testing. This requires a number of additional steps by the parent or guardian, including identifying and finding the laboratory, arranging for transportation to get there, taking time off from work, and finding child care for any other children who must remain at home, to name a few.

Reporting and Surveillance of Childhood Lead Poisoning in Allegheny County

Reporting the results of childhood blood lead screens is essential for two reasons: It expedites the case management and/or treatment of an individual child with an elevated blood lead level, and it provides the data necessary to characterize the epidemiology of elevated blood lead levels (PA DOH, 2005). Complete and accurate surveillance information about local lead poisoning risk factors can help guide development of appropriate screening recommendations, reinforce public education efforts regarding the importance of childhood screening, and encourage strategic partnerships for improving primary prevention efforts as well as screening and reporting.

Like most states, Pennsylvania has laboratory-reporting requirements to ensure that blood lead results are reported. However, a range of issues currently impedes reporting and surveillance processes in Allegheny County.

First, representatives of some state-licensed blood lead laboratories that serve health care providers in Allegheny County express difficulties associated with reporting electronically to PA-NEDSS using the specified HL7 format.

Second, many of the professionals involved in surveillance systems and at local laboratories report that health care providers are "notorious" for providing incomplete patient and/or lead test information on specimens sent for external processing and reporting. Some laboratories will follow up with providers to obtain the required information; others will report to PA-NEDSS only the information they are provided. In particular, the lack of Medicaid status information for blood lead specimen results entered into PA-NEDSS makes it impossible to reliably cross-reference PA-NEDSS data with Medicaid data. Since the Pennsylvania Department of Public Welfare (PA DPW) no longer collects blood lead levels for young children when they are screened, it can be difficult to identify children who require a follow-up evaluation.

Third, until recently, there have been very few staff within the PA DOH assigned to monitor blood lead level data and identify data integrity problems. The approach of the PA DOH has been to hold the laboratory responsible for complete information, but laboratory-licensing procedures do not include adequate review of adherence to reporting requirements for blood lead level screening.

Fourth, the local Medicaid MCOs interviewed indicate that historically the PA DPW OMAP has not aggressively monitored blood lead screening rates. Follow up for non-Medicaid children referred for blood lead screens who are not tested is more complicated, since there is no ready mechanism for others outside the provider's office to identify them.

Conclusions and Recommendations

The findings of this study suggest that current blood lead level reporting and surveillance data are inadequate for accurately assessing the true prevalence of childhood lead poisoning in Allegheny County or the number of children who are at risk for lead poisoning but have not yet been screened. Thus, there is a clear need for more diligent state and local involvement to ensure that at-risk children in Allegheny County are screened, and that the information is reported appropriately.

At the state level, we recommend the following long- and near-term actions by the public entities that have a mandate to address these issues. These entities include the PA DOH, PA DPW, the Pennsylvania Department of Insurance (PA DOI), the ACHD, and the Medicaid MCOs serving Allegheny County.

- Implement the PA DOH Lead Elimination Plan's recommendation to institute universal blood lead screening for *all* children at one and two years of age.
- The PA DPW Office of Child Development and the PA DOH should request that the PA DOI adopt the Medicaid blood lead screening requirements for children who are beneficiaries of the State Children's Health Insurance Program (SCHIP).
- The PA DOH and the PA DPW should use one integrated database (i.e., PA-NEDSS) for surveillance of childhood blood lead levels in Pennsylvania.

- The PA DOH should enforce the current requirements for blood lead reporting to PA-NEDSS, including standards of reporting that must be met by all state-licensed laboratories. At a minimum, the PA DOH should require that information on children's insurance include Medicaid identification.
- The PA DOH should also provide more extensive technical assistance and support to state-licensed blood lead laboratories on proper electronic reporting.
- The PA DPW should reinstitute the requirements for reporting blood lead levels for all Medicaid children who are screened, or explore other options for obtaining this information, such as utilizing PA-NEDSS data.
- The PA DPW OMAP should step up its efforts to aggressively monitor current Early and Periodic Screening, Diagnostic, and Treatment (EPSDT) program requirements for childhood blood lead level screening, establishing a goal of 90-percent compliance for MCOs in Allegheny County by 2006. Managed care contracts should be revised to include quality or performance standards relating specifically to lead.
- The PA DOH and the PA DPW should establish procedures for cross-referencing blood lead level surveillance data in the PA-NEDSS and Medicaid databases no later than July 2006.

At the county level, we recommend the following actions, to be implemented under the guidance of the ACHD.

- The ACHD, the Medicaid MCOs serving Allegheny County, and interested local organizations should enhance public education and awareness efforts targeted at parents and health care providers about the importance of repeat blood lead level screening at age two and the adverse effects of blood lead levels of 10 µg/dL or higher on early childhood neurodevelopment.
- Health care providers should also be educated on the validity of capillary draws. The PA DPW, the ACHD, and Medicaid MCOs should assume responsibility for ensuring that health care providers receive training and kits for in-house capillary specimen collection (including filter papers) and the export of specimens for all Medicaid-enrolled children to licensed blood lead laboratories. The ACHD and the PA DOH should strongly encourage the adoption of the same practices among private commercial insurers for all other children.
- The Pennsylvania Chapter of the AAP should add blood lead screening tests to the immunization records they provide to parents.
- ACHD should establish a two- to three-year pilot program with the Alliance for Infants and Toddlers (Alliance) for developmental screening and tracking of a sample of children with blood lead levels of 10 µg/dL or higher, thus offering these children the benefits of the developmental screening and tracking process already conducted by the Alliance.

- All Medicaid MCOs serving Allegheny County should send feedback reports to their network providers on individual Medicaid children not screened for lead poisoning, including comparative data on blood lead screening compliance rates across practices. For all other children, ACHD and SCHIP administrators should encourage health care providers to develop an internal tracking ("tickler") system for identifying individual children for whom a blood draw was ordered by an external lab but whose blood was not tested.

Acknowledgments

The authors acknowledge with appreciation the guidance and support of the state and local stakeholders who agreed to participate in the advisory group for this study. We also express our thanks to the many individuals who contributed important information through their participation in interviews and focus groups. Finally, we thank our reviewers, Harold Alan Pincus, Herbert Needleman, and Devra Davis for their thoughtful comments and suggestions on earlier drafts of this report.

This study was made possible through the support of Healthy Home Resources, a nonprofit organization in Pittsburgh, Pennsylvania, that supports communities and families in creating and maintaining healthy homes by addressing the rise in illnesses caused or complicated by the presence of indoor environmental hazards, including lead.

Abbreviations

AAP	American Academy of Pediatrics
ACHD	Allegheny County Health Department
Alliance	Alliance for Infants and Toddlers
BLL	blood lead level
CDC	Centers for Disease Control and Prevention
CLPPP	Childhood Lead Poisoning Prevention Program
CMS	Centers for Medicare and Medicaid Services
CRP	Center for Rural Pennsylvania
EPDST	Early and Periodic Screening, Diagnostic, and Treatment
FEP	free erythrocyte protoporphyrin
GAO	U.S. General Accounting Office, now U.S. Government Accountability Office
HCFA	Health Care Financing Administration
HHS	U.S. Department of Health and Human Services
HMO	health maintenance organization
HRSA	Health Resources and Services Administration
HUD	U.S. Department of Housing and Urban Development
MCO	managed care organization
µg/dL	micrograms per deciliter
NHANES	National Health and Nutrition Examination Survey
OMAP	Office of Medical Assistance Program

PA DOH	Pennsylvania Department of Health
PA DOI	Pennsylvania Department of Insurance
PA DPW	Pennsylvania Department of Public Welfare
PA-NEDSS	Pennsylvania National Electronic Disease Surveillance System
PPC	Pennsylvania Partnerships for Children
SCHIP	State Children's Health Insurance Program
WIC	Special Supplemental Nutrition Program for Women, Infants, and Children
ZPP	zinc protoporphyrin

CHAPTER ONE

Introduction

Lead poisoning is a serious, preventable environmental health threat to young children in many communities throughout the United States (AAP, Committee on Environmental Health, 1998). One of the key goals for U.S. public health policy included in the U.S. Department of Health and Human Services (HHS) *Healthy People 2010* report is the elimination of elevated blood lead levels in children (see HHS, 2000). Achievement of this goal will require improvements in three general areas: (1) lead poisoning prevention; (2) screening, reporting, and surveillance of childhood blood lead levels; and (3) treatment of childhood lead poisoning. The focus of this report is on screening, reporting, and surveillance, which are critical not only to the overall goal of eliminating lead poisoning, but to its prevention and treatment as well.

Fortunately, past prevention efforts, in particular the removal of lead from gasoline, have led to a decline in the number of young children nationwide with elevated blood lead levels. Between 1999 and 2002, 1.6 percent of all children one to five years old, or 310,000, had blood lead levels at or above the current recommended cutoff of 10 micrograms of lead per deciliter of blood (µg/dL), compared to 88.2 percent between 1976 and 1980 (CDC, 2005). Overall, the mean national blood lead level has dropped from 13.7 µg/dL between 1976 and 1980, to 2.3 µg/dL between 1991 and 1994, and to 1.6 µg/dL between 1999 and 2002 (Pirkle, 1994; CDC, 2005).

Despite this significant reduction in the number of children nationally between the ages of one and five years who have elevated blood lead levels, and the lower levels of blood lead observed, a number of issues continue to complicate effective eradication of this important public health problem.

First, the general perception that the problem of childhood lead poisoning has been resolved must be corrected. To place the rate of high lead levels (i.e., 1.6 percent of children nationwide) in context, the national prevalence rates for autism, childhood depression, and attention deficit hyperactivity disorder—other childhood health problems currently considered to be of critical concern—are 0.91 percent, 5 percent, and 3 to 5 percent, respectively (American Academy of Child and Adolescent Psychiatry, 2004a, 2004c, 2004b). Unlike these other conditions, however, the causes of childhood lead poisoning are known, and the condition is 100-percent preventable.

Second, recent national blood lead level data continue to show a clear racial disparity. Although the largest decrease in elevated blood lead levels (from 11.2 percent in 1991–1994 to 3.1 percent in 1999–2002) has been among non-Hispanic black children aged one to five years, this group of young children remains at greater risk for exposure to harmful lead levels than non-Hispanic white children (1.3 percent) and Mexican-American children (2.0 percent) in the same age range (CDC, 2005). The risk of elevated blood lead levels also remains higher for other subpopulations of young children, including children from low-income families and children who live in older homes (CDC, 1997).

Third, because most young children with elevated blood lead levels have no obvious symptoms at the time of exposure, the prevention, detection, assessment, and management of lead poisoning and associated risk factors rely entirely on the results of blood lead screening tests.

Fourth, the absence of obvious symptoms belies the negative impact that even low levels of blood lead (i.e., less than 10 µg/dL) can have on a young child's cognitive, intellectual, and neurodevelopmental outcomes, and the very serious implications that these outcomes have for broader issues of national concern, such as school readiness and educational achievement levels.

Fifth, although eliminating childhood lead poisoning remains a high priority on the national public health agenda, responsibility for ensuring that at-risk young children are screened for lead poisoning and that the results are reported to relevant authorities is often fragmented at the county level, hindering adequate prevention, surveillance, and treatment efforts. In Pennsylvania, for example, all blood lead screening results must be reported directly to the state's disease surveillance system by health care providers or state-licensed laboratories. The Allegheny County Health Department (ACHD) is no longer the first recipient of this data. Its current responsibility is limited to case management for those children identified as having elevated blood lead levels based on data reported at the state level.

For all of these reasons, now more than ever, effective screening, reporting, and surveillance of childhood lead poisoning requires the concerted, proactive, and coordinated effort of state and local public health officials, health care and health plan providers, community agencies, and parents. Such efforts are particularly important in communities with high rates of reported elevated blood lead levels or with inadequate data on the prevalence of elevated blood lead levels, as well as in communities with older housing, which increases the risk of young children's exposure to harmful lead levels.

Background on Lead Poisoning

Sources of Lead Poisoning

Lead-based house paint is the major source of childhood lead poisoning in the United States, followed by lead-contaminated dust and soil (Public Health Service, 1999). Lead was a major ingredient in most interior and exterior oil-based house paint before 1950 and was still used in some paints until 1978, when the production of lead paint was officially banned. The U.S. Department of Housing and Urban Development (HUD) estimates that three-quarters of pre-1980 housing units contain some lead-based paint; the likelihood, extent, and concentration of lead-based paint increase with the age of the building. House dust is often contaminated by lead-based paint that is peeling, deteriorating, or disturbed during home renovation or the preparation of painted surfaces for repainting without proper safeguards. Soil contamination can be traced back to deteriorating exterior paint or past widespread use of leaded gasoline.

Other, less common sources of lead in a young child's environment include lead-contaminated drinking water (where lead solder and, sometimes, lead pipes were used in the municipal water system, in the child's home, or both); dust residues from worn lead wheel weights on urban streets; old and imported toys or furniture painted with lead-based paint; certain ethnic, traditional, or home remedies that involve lead ingestion; and the clothing of parents whose work (e.g., car repair, industrial machinery, bridge construction, battery manufacture, smelting, foundries) or hobby (e.g., clay ceramic pottery, stained glass making) involves high levels of lead.

Impact of Lead Poisoning

Lead is a neurotoxin that when ingested can adversely affect the structural and/or functional components of the nervous system and cause serious harm to virtually every other system of the body (e.g., hematologic, endocrinologic, renal, reproductive). At extremely high levels (i.e., greater than 70 µg/dL), lead can cause seizures, coma, severe brain and kidney damage, and death. At lower levels (i.e., less than 10 µg/dL), lead can adversely impact cognition and intellectual functioning, particularly among young children (National Research Council, 1993; Needleman and Bellinger, 1989; Needleman and Gastonis, 1990; Baghurst et al, 1992; Bellinger, Stiles, and Needleman, 1992; McMichael et al, 1988; Needleman, Gunnoe et al, 1979; Needleman, Leviton, and Bellinger, 1982; Bellinger and Needleman, 2003). Clearly, the impact of even low levels of blood lead in young children has serious implications for school readiness and educational achievement levels. In 1991, concern was sufficient for HHS to revise the threshold at which blood lead levels are considered to be elevated, from the previous 25 µg/dL to 10 µg/dL.

Considerable controversy and debate continue in the public health policy arena concerning the precise threshold at which blood lead levels should be considered elevated. A recent five-year study has found that children who have blood lead concentrations lower than 10 μg/dL suffer intellectual impairment from the exposure, and that the marginal biological impact of a microgram of lead on a child's IQ is proportionally greater at levels below 10 μg/dL than at levels above (Canfield et al., 2003). Other studies have shown that with a cutoff limit of 5 μg/dL—half the threshold currently used by the Centers for Disease Control and Prevention (CDC) to define an elevated blood lead level—there are significant effects on the verbal, perceptual, and attention skills that are critical to future reading success of young children (Beaman, 1998). Experts in the field have long argued that no exposure to lead is safe and that millions more children are adversely affected by environmental lead than previously estimated.

Recent research has also been directed to other aspects of the developmental neurotoxicity of lead. Using instruments that provide valid and reliable measures of attention, behavior, and other aspects of neurodevelopment, associations have been identified between lead exposure and weaknesses in attention and vigilance, increased aggression, somatic complaints, and antisocial or delinquent behaviors (Bellinger, Titlebaum et al., 1994; Sciarillo, Alexander, and Farrell, 1992; Needleman, Riess et al., 1996). Other adverse neurodevelopmental effects that have been associated with low to moderate elevated blood lead levels include a reduction in auditory threshold, abnormal postural balance, poor eye-hand coordination, longer reaction times, and sleep disturbances (Robinson et al., 1987; Schwartz and Otto, 1987; Bhattacharya et al., 1990; Needleman, Gunnoe, and Leviton, 1979; Owens-Stively et al., 1997). Moreover, many other social factors that affect young children's health (e.g., socioeconomic status, single-parent household, teenaged mother, poor nutrition) have been shown to act in combination with lead hazards to exacerbate adverse health effects (Hubal et al., 2000).

To date, there is no empirical basis for recommending specific interventions for children with neurodevelopmental problems resulting from elevated blood lead levels. However, it is reasonable to assume that such children would benefit from the types of interventions shown to be effective in facilitating the development of other groups of children with similar problems. Given that some studies have found a stronger correlation between children's previous blood lead levels and their current neurodevelopmental status than between current levels and current neurodevelopmental status, careful long-term surveillance of neurodevelopment is needed to ensure that children in need of such interventions are identified.

The economic costs of lead poisoning are also significant. According to the CDC, medical spending for lead poisoning treatment totaled $3 billion in 1992, an average of $925 per case (CDC, National Center for Injury Prevention and Control, 2004). Moreover, for every dollar spent on poison-control services in 1992, an estimated $7 was saved in medical care payments by reducing the number of medically treated poisonings. The savings per poisoning call totaled $175. One recent county-level study conducted in Mahoning, Ohio, estimated case management and treatment costs for 279 children with elevated blood levels to be in the range of $500,000, or $1,800 per child (Stefanak et al., 2005).

Groups Most at Risk for Lead Poisoning

Lead is particularly hazardous to children under the age of six who absorb lead differently than adults, have still-developing nervous systems that are particularly vulnerable to lead, and engage in normal play activities that may expose them to lead-based paint and lead-contaminated dust and soil in multiple environments (e.g., child care centers, babysitters' residences, homes of relatives, playgrounds, schools).

Children under three years of age are particularly susceptible for two reasons. First, at this age, children are at a sensory-motor developmental stage where they explore and learn about their environment by crawling on floors, playing in grass, and putting nonfood objects into their mouths, thus increasing their contact with lead contaminants, indoors and out (University of Minnesota, 2004). Second, from birth to age three, the functional capacity of a child's brain undergoes exceedingly rapid development (Halfon, Shulman, and Hochstein, 2001). Since the synapses connecting the neurons and the myelin insulating them are not yet fully developed at birth, most of the brain's functional capacity does not begin to develop until after birth. Before the age of three, the number of synaptic connections in the young child's brain doubles to approximately 1,000 trillion, many more than will ultimately be present in the adult's brain. Consequently, at this stage of neurodevelopment, the neurotoxicity effects of lead are most severe.

Some subpopulations of young children are particularly at risk, including low-income and minority children and children who live in older housing (CDC, 2005; CDC, 1997; CDC, National Center for Health Statistics, 1995). Low-income children are defined as those of families receiving some form of government assistance (i.e., Medicaid, Special Supplemental Nutrition Program for Women, Infants, and Children [WIC]; Supplemental Security Income; welfare; or subsidized child care). The U.S. General Accounting Office (GAO) estimated that 60 percent of all children with blood lead levels greater than 10 µg/dL, and 83 percent of all children with blood lead levels greater than 20 µg/dL, are enrolled in Medicaid (GAO, 1999). Another report estimated that 535,000 Medicaid-enrolled children have elevated blood lead levels, a prevalence rate of 9 percent among one- to five-year-olds—a rate three times higher than that of children not enrolled in Medicaid (3 percent) (GAO, 1998). The most recent national blood lead level data for the 1999–2002 period shows that non-Hispanic black children one to five years old have the highest prevalence of elevated blood lead levels (3.1 percent) compared to other children in the same age group, with the prevalence among non-Hispanic white children and Mexican-American children at 1.3 percent and 2.0 percent, respectively (CDC, 2005).

Primary Preventions for Lead Poisoning

Primary prevention means controlling lead hazards before children are ever exposed to lead. As lead-based paint is the primary source of lead exposure in the United States, and high lead exposures occur most frequently where children spend the majority of their time, public health efforts to remove lead from children's residences and sites of routine care are a critical step in preventing childhood lead poisoning (PA DOH, 2005). Housing data from the U.S. Bureau of the Census, in combination with blood lead level surveillance data when available from screening, can help prevent lead exposure by targeting lead poisoning prevention activities to the neighborhoods and populations at highest risk in a particular area.

The CDC, the federal agency within HHS responsible for issuing recommendations for screening and treating young children for lead poisoning, recommends environmental investigation for venous lead levels of 20 µg/dL or higher and for those persistently above 15 µg/dL. No official recommendations have been published by the CDC regarding environmental investigation of cases in which children have blood lead levels of 15 µg/dL or less. According to PA DOH guidelines, a case should be closed for case management purposes if two confirmed blood lead levels below 10 µg/dL are drawn three months apart, or if three confirmed blood lead levels below 15 µg/dL are drawn three months apart (PA DOH, 2005)

Environmental lead removal techniques include residential paint-hazard remediation, high-efficiency particulate air vacuuming, interior dust abatement, and soil abatement. The efficacy of each technique varies depending on pre-abatement blood levels and frequency of intervention (or combined interventions) (Ellis and Kane, 2000). When lead hazard control work is required, parents and property owners should ensure that the work is done by trained professional contractors (PA DOH, 2005). If done properly, abatement work removes the immediate lead hazard that results in lead exposure. However, if done improperly, it can increase inhabitants' exposure to lead. Although this work can be expensive (i.e., an estimated $10,000 per unit), financing through local, state, and federal grant and loan programs may be available in many communities through health departments or housing offices (AAP, Committee on Environmental Health, 1998).

Other primary preventions, such as public education about the hazards of lead exposure, provision of anticipatory guidance by health care providers, and information about nutrition and the importance of dietary iron for preventing elevated blood lead levels, can further assist parents in taking measures to minimize their children's exposure to lead.

Secondary Preventions for Lead Poisoning

Secondary prevention is based on the identification of exposed children through a blood lead screening test, thereby reducing the duration, intensity, and consequences of lead exposure. Identification of children with lead poisoning can lead to treatment and interventions designed to reduce blood lead levels or prevent future exposures (Lane and Kemper, 2001; Charney et al., 1983; Rhoads et al., 1999; Schultz, Pawel, and Murphy, 1999). The proper management of children with confirmed (venous) blood lead levels higher than 10 µg/dL is based on the relative degree of the elevation (see Table 1.1).

Table 1.1
Summary of CDC Recommendations for Children with Confirmed (Venous) Elevated Blood Lead Levels

Blood Lead Level (µg/dL)				
10–14	15–19	20–44	45–69	70 or higher
Lead education: Dietary Environmental	Lead education: Dietary Environmental	Lead education: Dietary Environmental	Lead education: Dietary Environmental	Hospitalize and commence chelation therapy
Follow-up blood lead monitoring	Follow-up blood lead monitoring	Follow-up blood lead monitoring	Follow-up blood lead monitoring	Proceed according to actions for 45–69 µg/dL
	Proceed according to actions for 20–44 µg/dL if a follow-up BLL is in this range at least 3 months after initial venous test or BLLs increase	Complete history and physical exam Lab work: Hemoglobin or hematocrit Iron status	Complete history and physical exam Lab work: Hemoglobin or hematocrit Iron status FEP or ZPP	
		Environmental investigation	Environmental investigation	
		Lead hazard reduction	Lead hazard reduction	
		Neuro-developmental monitoring	Neuro-developmental monitoring	
		Abdominal X-ray (if particulate lead ingestion is suspected) with bowel decontamination if indicated	Abdominal X-ray with bowel decontamination if indicated	
			Chelation therapy	

NOTES: BLL = blood lead level. FEP = free erythrocyte protoporphyrin. ZPP = zinc protoporphyrin.

The CDC recommends a coordinated program of follow-up screenings, education, case management, environmental investigation, lead hazard control, and clinical evaluation (see Table 1.1) (CDC, 2002). These guidelines are not intended for use as a complete protocol but rather as a tool for adapting the management of childhood lead poisoning to local needs and conditions. The recommendations of the American Academy of Pediatrics (AAP) are consistent with those of the CDC (AAP, Committee on Environmental Health, 1998). Several states have also published case management and treatment guidelines to assist health care providers and public health personnel in managing children with elevated blood lead levels. Standards produced by the Pennsylvania Department of Health (PA DOH) for ensuring that comprehensive services are provided to families of children with elevated blood lead levels are presented in Table 1.2 (PA DOH, 2005). A useful office-based approach to management for the clinician has also recently been published (Feingold and Anderson, 2004).

Elimination of Childhood Lead Poisoning Remains a National and State Public Health Priority

Addressing the problem of childhood lead poisoning remains a high priority on the national and state public health agendas. In 1991, HHS published a 15-year strategic plan calling for the elimination of childhood lead poisoning by the year 2011 (HHS, 1991). The plan identified universal screening of children and abatement of all lead

Table 1.2
PA DOH Standards for Services to Be Provided to Families of Children with Elevated Blood Lead Levels

PA DOH Standard	Services to Be Provided
Standard 1	Parents/guardians who have children with confirmed venous blood lead levels of 10 to 14 µg/dL should receive educational materials from a public health professional.
Standard 2	All children with confirmed initial venous blood lead levels of 15 to 19 µg/dL will be referred for follow-up by a public health official to ensure that a second venous blood lead level is obtained within three months.
Standard 3	All children with confirmed venous blood lead levels of 20 to 44 µg/dL or two consecutive blood lead levels of 15 to 19 µg/dL (within a three-month time frame) will be referred to a public health professional for case management, home visits, and an environmental investigation.
Standard 4	All children with confirmed venous blood lead levels of 45 to 69 µg/dL will be referred to a public health professional for case management, home visits, and an environmental investigation. The public health professional will refer the child to a primary care provider for evaluation for chelation therapy.
Standard 5	All children with confirmed venous blood lead levels of 70 µg/dL or higher will be referred to a public health professional for case management, home visits, and an environmental investigation. The public health professional will make every effort to assure that all children are referred to a primary care provider for hospitalization for chelation therapy.

paint in housing built before 1950 as essential parts of a national strategy to eliminate childhood lead poisoning. A strong national effort developed to eliminate the disease, but was derailed by prevailing attitudes and opposition from many directions, including the lead industry, realtors, landlords, insurance companies, some health maintenance organizations (HMOs), and a small number of pediatricians in private practice (Needleman, 1998). In its fiscal year 1999 performance plan to Congress, HHS reiterated its previous commitment by including the elimination of childhood lead poisoning as one of the objectives for the CDC. Among its departmentwide *Healthy People 2010* objectives, HHS also established the goal of no children between the ages of one and five with blood lead levels exceeding 10 µg/dL.

Likewise, the Commonwealth of Pennsylvania has identified lead poisoning as a significant health concern for Pennsylvania's children, and the PA DOH Childhood Lead Poisoning Prevention Program (CLPPP)[1] has developed a Lead Elimination Plan to ensure that all children in the Commonwealth are free from lead poisoning (PA DOH, 2005). The Pennsylvania CLPPP surveillance subcommittee's recommendation calls for universal screening of all children at the age of one and two years, and for all children aged three through six years without a confirmed prior blood lead test. The subcommittee found that universal screening is indicated according to the CDC criteria and based on the higher prevalence of both elevated blood lead levels in Pennsylvania children and the abundance of pre-1950 housing found in the Commonwealth.

Local city or county recommendations should be followed when they are more stringent than state recommendations. The Allegheny County Health Department is recommending the screening of all children at the age of one and two years.

Other CLPPP subcommittees have issued detailed recommendations regarding the detection and abatement of lead hazards in residential properties, the development or modification of educational materials, and the dissemination of case management manuals to health care providers.

Special Issues Related to Lead Poisoning in Pittsburgh and Allegheny County

Pittsburgh ranks 28th on the CDC's list of the 129 cities with the greatest number of children estimated to have elevated blood lead levels (PA DOH, 2005). The CDC

---

[1] The Lead Contamination Control Act of 1988 authorized the CDC to initiate program efforts to eliminate childhood lead poisoning in the United States. As a result, the CDC Childhood Lead Poisoning Prevention Branch was created in 1990. One of its primary responsibilities is to provide funding to state and local health departments in order to determine the extent of childhood lead poisoning by screening children for elevated blood lead levels, help ensure that lead-poisoned infants and children receive medical and environmental follow-up, and develop neighborhood-based efforts to prevent childhood lead poisoning. In 2003, the CDC awarded $31.7 million to 42 state and local health departments, including the PA DOH and the ACHD, to develop and implement comprehensive lead poisoning prevention programs.

and the AAP recommend that communities with comparable blood lead levels institute universal, rather than targeted or selected, blood lead screening. Moreover, many children in Allegheny County belong to high-risk groups. Data from the 2000 U.S. Census show that there are 71,081 children under the age of six in Allegheny County, and approximately 17 percent of them live in households that are below the poverty level. In addition, 31,832 children in Allegheny County under the age of five live in census tracts where the median-year housing was built before 1950 (U.S. Census Bureau, 2000a; 2000b) (see Appendix A). The total number of one- and two-year-old Medicaid recipients who should have been screened for lead poisoning far exceeds the number of blood lead screening tests reported, suggesting that blood lead screening for Medicaid children in Allegheny County, as elsewhere in the United States, remains suboptimal.

Study Purpose and Methodology

In light of the continued public health importance of blood lead poisoning among children under six years of age, the critical role that lead screening can play in both its prevention and treatment, and the questions raised above regarding the screening of young children at risk for elevated blood lead levels in Allegheny County, the RAND Corporation, in collaboration with the University of Pittsburgh Office of Child Development, was commissioned by Healthy Home Resources to do the following:

- Review the quality of existing data on blood lead screening, reporting, and surveillance for young children in Allegheny County, and, if feasible, use this data for estimating (1) the prevalence of childhood lead poisoning in Allegheny County and (2) the number of young children in Allegheny County with blood lead levels of 10 μg/dL or greater who have not been screened.
- Identify key barriers to screening, reporting, and surveillance efforts in Allegheny County, and potential strategies for overcoming them.
- Develop a set of recommendations for improving screening, reporting, and surveillance in Allegheny County.

An ancillary task was to determine how Allegheny County's childhood lead poisoning prevalence and blood lead screening rates compare to those of other regions with similar levels of risk, also based on existing screening, reporting, and surveillance data. We note that an assessment of efforts for enhancing primary prevention activities (such as lead hazard control work) and ensuring appropriate case management and treatment for children with elevated blood lead levels are outside the scope of this study.

To meet the study objectives, between July 2004 and June 2005, the RAND–University of Pittsburgh project team conducted a background study of the relevant literature; a review of existing childhood blood lead level reporting and surveillance databases for Pennsylvania and Allegheny County; and interviews and focus groups with national, state, and local stakeholders.

The background study of the literature was designed to provide a foundation of knowledge upon which to conduct subsequent analyses of the screening, reporting, and surveillance processes in Allegheny County and to formulate recommendations for improving these processes. Relevant legislation, policy documents, and research studies were reviewed to gather information on national, state, and local guidelines and mandates for childhood blood lead level screening and reporting, as well as the locus of responsibility for enforcing them; known barriers to effective screening, reporting, and surveillance of childhood blood lead levels; best-practice models for enhancing screening, reporting, and surveillance of childhood blood lead levels, especially for at-risk populations; and emerging research findings on the impact of low to moderate blood lead levels on young children's neurodevelopmental outcomes.

Three extant databases containing information on childhood lead poisoning in Pennsylvania and Allegheny County were examined: the National Health and Nutrition Examination Survey (NHANES), the Pennsylvania National Electronic Disease Surveillance System (PA-NEDSS), and the Pennsylvania Medicaid database. In each case, we explored the following questions: What types of data are available? How comprehensive are the available data? What are the limitations of the data? Given the strengths and weaknesses of the existing data, what conclusions, if any, can be drawn from them about blood lead poisoning among young children in Allegheny County? In particular, can estimates be made regarding the number of children under age six in Allegheny County with blood lead levels of 10 µg/dL or greater, including those who have not been screened? Finally, how do Allegheny County's blood lead screening rates and prevalence rates for childhood lead poisoning compare with those of other regions with similar risk factors for childhood lead poisoning?

The interviews and focus groups were designed to elicit experts' views on current screening, reporting, and surveillance efforts in Allegheny County, Pennsylvania, and elsewhere, and to identify barriers to these processes in Allegheny County and potential strategies for overcoming them. In total, the project team conducted 15 interviews with the appropriate representatives from one local health clinic, two state-licensed blood lead laboratories in Allegheny County (one large and one small), two local Medicaid physical health managed care organizations (MCOs), the ACHD, the PA DOH, the Pennsylvania Department of Public Welfare (PA DPW) Office of Medical Assistance Program (OMAP), the CDC, one CLPPP in another Pennsylvania county, and one CLPPP in another state. We also conducted two focus groups with parents from two family centers in at-risk communities in Allegheny County; one focus group had eight parents and the other had nine.

The project team also established a 16-person advisory group for this study that met three times during the study period (in September 2004, January 2005, and April 2005) to review the project goals and tasks, discuss the preliminary findings, and refine the proposed recommendations, respectively (see Appendix B).

About This Report

This report provides a synthesis of the study findings, with each chapter integrating relevant information from the background study of the literature, database analyses, and interviews and focus groups, as appropriate. Chapter Two provides a review of existing blood lead level screening, reporting, and surveillance data relevant to Allegheny County, including estimates of childhood lead poisoning prevalence in Allegheny County and the number of young children in Allegheny County with blood lead levels of 10 µg/dL or higher who have not been screened. Chapters Three and Four examine the screening and reporting/surveillance processes in Allegheny County, respectively, with a particular focus on the barriers that currently impede these processes and potential strategies for overcoming them. Chapter Five concludes with a set of recommendations for improving childhood blood lead level screening, reporting, and surveillance in Allegheny County, Pennsylvania.

CHAPTER TWO

Existing Data on Childhood Blood Lead Screening, Reporting, and Surveillance in Allegheny County

A primary task of this study was to review the quality of existing data on blood lead screening, reporting, and surveillance for children under the age of six in Allegheny County, and, if feasible, use this data for estimating the prevalence of childhood lead poisoning in Allegheny County and the number of young children in Allegheny County with blood lead levels of 10 µg/dL or higher who have not been screened. An ancillary task was to compare Allegheny County's childhood lead poisoning prevalence and blood lead screening rates to those of other regions with similar levels of risk, also based on existing screening, reporting, and surveillance data.

In this chapter, we describe the data characteristics and quality of the three blood lead level screening, reporting, and surveillance databases that were analyzed to complete these tasks; present the information that we were able to obtain from them, both individually and collectively; and, based on this information, offer the estimates of childhood lead poisoning prevalence and the number of children not screened, as described above. This analysis was informed by the background study of the literature and interviews with state and local stakeholders, primarily those involved in blood lead level data collection, reporting, and surveillance.

Descriptions of Existing Databases and the Information They Provide About Allegheny County

Data on blood lead testing from three extant databases were examined: the National Health and Nutrition Examination Survey (NHANES); the Pennsylvania National Electronic Disease Surveillance System (PA-NEDSS); and the Pennsylvania Medicaid database. Each database was analyzed with regard to data characteristics (e.g., years in which data were collected, population in database, source of data, ages of children analyzed for this study, types of data available, and whether blood lead level data were reported) and data quality (e.g., strengths and weaknesses of the data) (see Tables 2.1 and 2.2).

Table 2.1
Data Characteristics of Existing Blood Lead Screening Databases

Data Characteristic	NHANES	PA-NEDSS	EPSDT
Collecting entity	Centers for Disease Control and Prevention (CDC)	PA Department of Health	PA Office of Medical Assistance (Medicaid)
Year data collected	1999–2000	2004–2005	2000–2001
Population in database	National random sample of 9,928 children from 44 states, NYC, and DC	Children in Pennsylvania for whom lab work has been done for one of the 61 reportable diseases	All Medicaid children birth–20 years old who have had an EPSDT screen
Source of data	CDC labs	All labs servicing PA	Claims data for Medicaid MCOs and fee-for-service programs
Ages of children analyzed for this study	Under 72 months of age	Under 72 months of age	Under 72 months of age
Types of data available	Blood lead levels (all venous draws)	Blood lead levels plus lab results for 60 of the 72 reportable diseases	Lab results for all EPSDT screens, including hearing, vision, immunizations, and lead testing
Blood lead level data reported?	Yes	Yes	No

Table 2.2
Quality of Data in Existing Blood Lead Screening Databases

Data Characteristic	NHANES	PA-NEDSS	EPSDT
Strengths of the data	• Population-based • High control over samples and analyses (all done by CDC staff and labs) • 100% venous draws	• Population-based electronic reporting • Data from state-licensed labs • PA DOH staff beginning to review data for quality	• Known demographic information • Known volume of anticipated reports • Can do checks to determine who is missing lead screens
Weaknesses of the data	• National sample restricts predictions to areas smaller than national level	• Unknown volume of anticipated reports by lab and individual • No enforcement of mandated reporting by labs • No match with EPSDT dataset • No enforcement of presence and/or accuracy of some mandated data points	• No enforcement of mandated screening by CMS or OMAP (accepts 50% screening rates) • No enforcement of mandated reporting by labs • Reliant on claims data known to be underreported • EPSDT screens can be done without lead test • No blood lead levels reported

NOTE: EPSDT = Early and Periodic Screening, Diagnostic, and Treatment.

National Health and Nutrition Examination Survey (NHANES)

The NHANES, conducted multiple times since 1960 by the CDC National Center for Health Statistics, is a longitudinal study designed to provide national estimates of the health and nutrition status of the noninstitutionalized U.S. civilian population over the age of two months. It consists of a random sample of adults and children from 44 states (Pennsylvania included), New York City, and Washington, D.C. Data are collected annually using multiple methodologies, such as phone interviews, food diaries, and blood work conducted via venous draws by CDC staff and analyzed by CDC laboratories. Data used for the current study were from 1999–2002 blood lead level reports of 1,160 children representing 90.1 percent of the total random sample of children between the ages of one and five years.

The NHANES sample selection process and overall study methodology ensure the reliability of its results for the nation as a whole. However, the ability to use this data to make predictions regarding local prevalence rates is limited. At best, these data provide an *approximate* range of the number of children with elevated blood lead levels in Allegheny County.

With this in mind, the project team used the NHANES data to provide a baseline for the prevalence of blood lead levels 10 μg/dL or greater for all children ages one to five years, as well as Medicaid children under the age of six years, in Allegheny County. Based on NHANES national prevalence rates (1.6 percent for a sample of all children; 9 percent for a subsample of Medicaid children[1]), U.S. Bureau of the Census data for Allegheny County in 2000, and average monthly Medicaid enrollment data for 2003, 1,156 young children in Allegheny County are estimated to have blood lead levels of 10 μg/dL or higher, and 2,268 young Medicaid children in Allegheny County are estimated to have blood lead levels of 10 μg/dL or higher.

Clearly, these two numbers are incongruent and cannot be reconciled (i.e., the number of Medicaid-enrolled children in Allegheny County with elevated blood lead levels cannot be larger than the total number of children in Allegheny County with elevated blood lead levels). One obvious reason for this incongruence is that the prevalence rates are based on two different sets of data. Although the CDC has published NHANES survey data showing a drop in the prevalence rates for elevated blood lead levels among all children (i.e., from 8.6 percent in 1988–1994 to 1.6 percent in 1999–2001), it has not yet made available comparable data for the subsample of Medicaid-enrolled children.

Pennsylvania National Electronic Disease Surveillance System (PA-NEDSS)

The National Electronic Disease Surveillance System is an initiative led by the CDC that promotes the use of data and information system standards to advance the development of efficient, integrated, and interoperable surveillance systems at federal, state,

---

[1] Medicaid data is based on 1988–1994 state-level NHANES data that have not been updated.

and local levels. It is a major component of the Public Health Information Network—the CDC's vision for advancing fully capable real-time information systems that allow prompt follow-up by the many organizations that participate in public health, assuming that the necessary data is submitted.

Based on the national system created by the CDC, PA-NEDSS is an award-winning system of electronic reporting that allows the PA DOH to identify, manage, and treat 61 of the 72 reportable diseases in the state, including lead poisoning. As of November 16, 2003, PA-NEDSS became the mandatory electronic disease-reporting application for the Commonwealth. All state-licensed laboratories are required to manually or electronically report laboratory results on the 61 diseases for all Pennsylvania residents irrespective of insurance status.

PA-NEDSS has significant potential for providing public health professionals and other health care providers with population-based and individual-specific electronic data that is comprehensive, timely, and of high quality. However, PA DOH staff have only recently been added to implement a quality-review process for the blood lead component. Moreover, at present, all of the data elements required by regulation do not have to be provided in order for the blood lead specimen results to be accepted in the blood lead database. Consequently, a good deal of "required" information is currently missing. The PA DOH believes that, at this point in time, incomplete data is better than "dummy" data that might be provided simply to complete a mandated data point. In addition, the completeness of reporting on blood lead level screening is difficult to measure since there is an unknown volume of anticipated reports by laboratories (i.e., the database is not pre-populated with birth data). Nor can the database currently be cross-referenced with Medicaid data.

As of 2003, there were 33,708 blood lead levels reported for children ages one to five years in Pennsylvania, including blood lead levels for 3,606 children in Allegheny County. There is currently a backlog of 2004 data to be entered; as of April 11, 2005, there were blood lead levels for 3,321 children ages one to five years in Allegheny County for 2004.

Medicaid/Early and Period Screening, Diagnostic, and Treatment (EPSDT)

The Medicaid program, administered by the Health Care Financing Administration (HCFA), is a major health care financing program for low-income families. Medicaid is a joint federal and state program that funds medical care for about one-third of all U.S. children between the ages of one and five. The Early and Periodic Screening, Diagnostic, and Treatment (EPSDT) service, administered through OMAP, is Medicaid's comprehensive and preventive health care program for individuals under the age of 21. EPSDT provides children with medical checkups consisting of a complete physical exam and immunizations; hearing and vision tests; developmental screening; lab work, including blood lead tests; complete health history; and educational materials on preventive health care practices. Parents can utilize all or some of these components at no cost, and participation is not enforced. Parents who elect not to have their children screened for lead poisoning, for example, are not required to show that a lead screening was completed elsewhere.

For this study, we examined a subset of Medicaid claims data on eligible children under six years of age for whom the data indicated that an EPSDT screening had been conducted during fiscal year 2000–2001. These data were obtained from Medicaid physical health MCOs and fee-for-service recipients. For these children, the blood lead data indicate only that a lead screening was completed and a claim submitted. The data do not specify blood lead levels for children screened or whether the blood lead levels were elevated. We note that several key informants reported that local claims data underrepresent the number of blood lead screenings completed in Allegheny County.

On the other hand, to its advantage, the Medicaid database does include the ages of all children enrolled in Medicaid, and, if applicable, their physical health MCOs and primary care providers. Thus, the relevant MCO and/or OMAP can determine which Medicaid children are missing a lead screening (based on date of birth and claims data) and then follow up as needed to encourage that blood lead level screenings be conducted in compliance with Medicaid requirements.

Comparisons Between Allegheny County and Other Areas with Comparable Levels of Risk for Childhood Lead Poisoning

In order to compare Allegheny County's screening and prevalence rates for childhood lead poisoning with those of other regions that have comparable levels of risk for childhood lead poisoning, we first examined the percent of the population in urban and rural areas[2] and the availability of specific health resources (i.e., a CLPPP and a local health department) for all counties in Pennsylvania (PPC, 2004). Next, we considered other demographics, such as median household income, the number of children under age six living in poverty, and the median age of housing. Through these assessments, we identified 11 counties in Pennsylvania that are comparable to Allegheny County: Berks, Chester, Dauphin, Erie, Lackawanna, Lancaster, Lehigh, Luzerne, Montgomery, Philadelphia, and York. Based on information provided in our national-level interviews and a similar set of analyses, Rhode Island was added as a comparable region outside the state with very similar demographics to Allegheny County.

The next step was to compare levels of risk based on specific risk factors, screening rates, and reported prevalence rates for lead poisoning in Allegheny County and

---

[2] Pennsylvania Partnerships for Children (PPC) uses the Center for Rural Pennsylvania (CRP) criteria for counties in their work with child welfare indicators. According to CRP categorization, counties with 75 percent or greater urbanized population are classified as urban, and counties with a 50 to 74 percent urbanized population are classified as urban mixed.

the other 11 Pennsylvania counties and Rhode Island. To make these comparisons, we relied on PA-NEDSS and Medicaid data for the 12 counties in Pennsylvania, including Allegheny County, and published literature and interviews for Rhode Island.

Levels of Risk

Levels of risk were determined by median household income in 1999, percent of children under the age of six years living in poverty, median age of housing, and percent of houses built before 1950. Appendix C provides complete data on the risk factors for all 12 Pennsylvania counties and Rhode Island. The highest level of risk for each factor is ranked 13. Allegheny County ranks ninth for median household income and percentage of children under six living in poverty, and tenth for median age of housing and percentage of houses built before 1950. These rankings are most similar to those of Erie County and in between those of Rhode Island and Philadelphia County for these four risk factors. Table 2.3 provides the data and rankings for these four regions. Interestingly, although all four regions have fairly similar risk profiles, based on existing data, they appear to have very different childhood blood lead screening rates, as explained below.

Table 2.3
Comparison of Risk Factors for Lead Poisoning Across Allegheny, Erie, and Philadelphia Counties and Rhode Island

Risk Factor	Allegheny County	Erie County	Philadelphia County	Rhode Island
Total population	1,281,666	280,843	1,517,550	1,048,319
Total children under 6 years old	86,511	21,144	118,695	76,798
Median household income (range = $65,295–$30,746)	$38,329 9th	$36,627 10th	$30,746 13th	$42,090 7th
Number of children under 6 years old in poverty	14,742	3,799	38,114	14,548
% of children under 6 years old in poverty (range = 4.9%–32.1%)	17.0% 9th	18.0% 10th	32.1% 13th	18.9% 12th
Median age of housing (range = 1973–1942)	1952 10th	1957 9th	1945 12th	1958 7th
% of houses built before 1950 (range = 20.5%–58.4%)	45.5% 10th	39.4% 8th	58.4% 13th	39.2% 7th

SOURCE: U.S. Census Bureau (2000a; 200b).

Lead Screening Rates

When comparisons are made based on the percentage of children under the age of six years who have received a lead screening as reported by PA-NEDSS for 2003,[3] the range of children screened varies from 15.3 percent for Erie County to 2 percent for both Lancaster and Chester Counties (see Table 2.4). Allegheny County ranks in the middle, or sixth, with 5.4 percent of young children screened. This is a lower screening rate than that for Erie County, which ranks first with 15.3 percent of young children screened for lead poisoning, and Philadelphia County, which ranks second with 10.6 percent of young children screened. However, children in all three of these counties in Pennsylvania are being screened at a much lower rate than Rhode Island's 87 percent.[4] We note that some of this discrepancy may be due in part to the current limitations of the PA-NEDSS blood lead component as described previously.

Table 2.4
Comparison of Screening Rates Based on PA-NEDSS 2003

County	Children Screened Before 72 Months (%)	Rank
Allegheny	5.4	6
Berks	7.8	4
Chester	2.0	12
Dauphin	5.3	7
Erie	15.3	1
Lackawanna	8.3	3
Lancaster	2.0	11
Lehigh	5.1	8
Luzerne	6.9	5
Montgomery	2.2	10
Philadelphia	10.6	2
York	4.1	9
Pennsylvania	**5.2**	—

[3] Though the current study has data as of April 11, 2005, for Allegheny County (see Table 2.1), Tables 2.3 and 2.4 present 2003 data when comparing Allegheny County to comparable counties since this data is complete. As noted previously, a backlog in inputting lead screenings conducted in 2004 for all of Pennsylvania is one reason for the incomplete 2004 data set.

[4] This rate was reported in the literature and confirmed during a telephone interview.

We also used Medicaid/EPSDT data to compare screening rates across the 12 comparable Pennsylvania counties for children enrolled in Medicaid during the 2000–2001 fiscal year (see Table 2.5). However, the strength of these comparisons is limited for two reasons. First, the data provided by Medicaid is a subset of all lead screening that occurred in Pennsylvania; and, second, there are local concerns that the current data may underreport the number of Medicaid blood lead screenings actually conducted in Allegheny County. These caveats notwithstanding, based on the data available, Allegheny County's screening rate for children enrolled in Medicaid is fifth among the 12 Pennsylvania counties.

Table 2.5
Comparison of Screening Rates Based on EPSDT 2000–2001

County	% EPSDT with Lead Screens	Rank	% Medicaid-Enrolled Children with EPSDT with Lead Screens	Rank
Allegheny	39.7	6	21.9	5
Berks	49.0	1	25.1	3
Chester	19.1	12	8.4	12
Dauphin	36.9	8	14.1	8
Erie	45.1	4	26.2	1
Lackawanna	44.4	5	25.4	2
Lancaster	31.7	11	13.0	11
Lehigh	33.3	9	17.5	7
Luzerne	46.2	2	23.8	4
Montgomery	32.2	10	14.0	9
Philadelphia	46.0	3	20.6	6
York	38.7	7	13.6	10

Prevalence Rates for Lead Poisoning

A comparison of the blood lead levels reported in PA-NEDSS for 2003 for the comparable counties in Pennsylvania shows that Allegheny County has a prevalence rate of 5.9 percent for children screened under the age of six years with blood lead levels of 10 μg/dL or greater, ranking fourth lowest among the 12 counties. However, there is very little difference in the prevalence rates for the four lowest ranking counties; higher rankings are associated with higher prevalence rates of lead poisoning (see Table 2.6). The range of prevalence rates is 5 percent for Chester County to 22 percent for Lancaster County. Erie County ranks seventh with a prevalence rate of 7.8 percent, and Philadelphia County ranks tenth with a prevalence rate of 17.7 percent.

We note that in Rhode Island, the prevalence rate for lead poisoning declined to below 4 percent in 2003 from more than 14 percent a decade ago.[5]

Table 2.6
Comparison of Children with Elevated Blood Lead Levels Based on PA-NEDSS 2003

County	Screened (n)	BLLs Above 10 μg/dL (n)	BLLs Above 10 μg/dL (of those screened) (%)	Rank (by %)	Predicted Population with BLLs >10 μg/dL (n)
Allegheny	4,641	274	5.9	4	5,091
Berks	2,197	203	9.2	8	2,593
Chester	697	35	5.0	1	1,786
Dauphin	991	183	18.5	11	3,459
Erie	3,249	253	7.8	7	1,650
Lackawanna	1,131	77	6.8	5	929
Lancaster	803	177	22.0	12	8,714
Lehigh	72	4	5.6	3	1,265
Luzerne	889	64	7.2	6	1,390
Montgomery	1,273	70	5.5	2	3,141
Philadelphia	12,651	2240	17.7	10	21,134
York	207	24	11.6	9	3,283
Pennsylvania	**45,784**	**5016**	**11.0**	—	**96,852**

---

[5] These rates were reported by a Rhode Island health official to a legislative panel considering regulations to tighten lead hazard rules for landlords.

Given that the available data reflect such a small percentage of children screened (2 to 15.3 percent), it is not possible to compare the actual prevalence of childhood lead poisoning or the efficiency of the screening process across these regions. For example, we do not know that Lancaster and Philadelphia Counties have more of a problem with lead poisoning, while Allegheny County has less of a problem, or that the responsible agencies in Lancaster and Philadelphia Counties do a better job of identifying and screening at-risk children than does Allegheny County. We do know, however, that of the small percentage of children under the age of six years whom Allegheny County reported to the PA-NEDSS database as having been screened (5.4 percent), 5.9 percent had blood lead levels of 10 µg/dL or greater.[6] In addition, fewer young children in Allegheny County are reported by state-licensed blood lead laboratories to PA-NEDSS as screened than are reported to the PA DPW OMAP, which is of concern since the Medicaid data are a subset of all children screened.

Estimating the Extent of Lead Poisoning Among Children in Allegheny County Who Have Not Been Screened

Given the limitations of the data described above, one cannot know with certainty the extent of the childhood lead poisoning problem in Allegheny County. Current inadequacies with regard to Pennsylvania surveillance data in particular make it impossible to determine whether the rate of elevated blood lead levels among young children in Allegheny County has declined to the same extent as the rates observed in national samples. Also unclear is the extent of elevated blood lead levels among young children in Allegheny County who have not been screened.

One estimate of the number of young children in Allegheny County with elevated blood lead levels who have not been screened can be derived utilizing current NHANES data and the PA-NEDSS report. The NHANES data indicate that 1.6 percent of all young children screened have blood lead levels of 10 µg/dL or greater. In Allegheny County, there are 72,220 children between the ages of one and five years, so it is reasonable to estimate that 1.6 percent of this total number (1,156) of young children also have blood lead levels of 10 µg/dL or greater. Combining this estimate with the PA-NEDSS data identifying 169 young children in Allegheny County with elevated blood lead levels yields an estimate of 987 children between the ages of one and five with elevated blood lead levels who have not been screened. If the national sample is reflective of the prevalence of blood lead levels in young children in Allegheny County, young African-American children are overrepresented in the subsample of 1,156 children predicted to elevated blood lead levels.

---

[6] The prevalence rate based on data through April 11, 2005, is 5.1 percent for the sample of 3,321 children ages one to five years.

The most current NHANES data do not include an updated analysis of the prevalence rate of elevated blood lead levels among young children with Medicaid benefits. Previous NHANES samples indicate that these children are most at risk for elevated blood lead levels, with 9 percent of those screened having blood lead levels of 10 µg/dL or greater. Based on data provided by the PA OMAP, only 40 percent of young children with Medicaid benefits in Allegheny County are reported to have had their blood lead levels assessed during their EPSDT screenings. Thus, 60 percent of these children have no reported blood lead level screens. In addition, the Pennsylvania Medicaid data do not include the actual blood lead level reported. If the historic 9-percent prevalence rate for this population is applicable to the current situation in Allegheny County, then 9 percent of the unscreened children with Medicaid benefits have elevated blood lead levels (i.e., 1,771 children under 72 months old).

Details related to both of the above estimates are presented in Table 2.7. It is important to underscore the critical point that the limitations of the existing data mean that these are estimates only—estimates derived using two different methods, two different national prevalence studies, and two different sets of Pennsylvania surveillance data. This process was necessary because of (1) the failure to complete blood lead level testing during the Medicaid EPSDT screening for 60 percent of the children receiving this benefit, or the underreporting of blood lead level screening for these children; (2) the dramatic underreporting of blood lead level screenings via PA-NEDSS for all children; and (3) the need to rely on national survey data regarding the prevalence of elevated blood lead levels given the inadequacy and/or incompleteness of local blood lead level screening and/or data reporting.

Table 2.7
Estimates of Prevalence Rates for Childhood Lead Poisoning in Allegheny County and the Number of Children in Allegheny County with Blood Lead Levels of 10 µg/dL or Greater Who Have Not Been Screened

	All Children		Medicaid and High-Risk Children	
	NHANES	**PA-NEDSS**	**EPSDT Allegheny County**	**EPSDT Pennsylvania**
Findings				
Year data collected	1999–2002	April 11, 2005	2000–2001 fiscal year	2002–2003 fiscal year
Population description	Children in U.S. 1–5 years of age	Children in Allegheny County 1–5 years of age	Medicaid children in Allegheny County under 72 months of age	Medicaid children in Pennsylvania under 72 months of age
Number in population	Unknown[a]	72,220	25,195	312,400
Number screened	1,160	3,321	5,513	133,434
Percentage of population screened	89.2% for entire U.S. sample age 1 and under[a]	4.6%	21% 40% with EPSDT screen	43%[d] 65% with EPSDT screen
Percentage screened with BLL 10 µg/dL or higher	1.6% all 1.3% Caucasian 3.1% African-American	5.1%[b] (n = 169)	Unknown (9% based on 1988–1994 NHANES data)[c]	Unknown (9% based on 1988–1994 NHANES data)[c]
Estimates for Allegheny County				
n children with blood lead levels 10 µg/dL or higher	1,156	3,683	2,268	2,268
n children with elevated blood lead levels not screened	987	3,514	1,1771	1,292[d]

[a] Not reported: how many children in the study aged 1–5 years who were not screened for blood lead levels.
[b] Rate from 2003 for children 1–5 years old was 6.9 percent of children tested who had blood lead levels of 10 µg/dL or higher.
[c] These data were not updated by the CDC.
[d] For children under three years of age, the testing rate is 63 percent, which translates to 839 children missed.

CHAPTER THREE

Screening for Childhood Lead Poisoning in Allegheny County

Although complete and reliable data for assessing the prevalence and subsequent risk of childhood lead poisoning in Allegheny County are currently lacking, the findings presented in Chapter Two suggest that ample opportunity exists to improve local screening rates. Blood lead screening is a relatively simple procedure that can be conducted in a health care provider's office, health center, or other primary care site. However, under a policy of targeted screening, the appropriateness of conducting a blood lead screening test may vary according to the risk level of the child and local conditions.

In this chapter, we present current federal, state, and local childhood blood lead screening requirements and recommendations, describe the screening process at the level of the individual child in Allegheny County, and discuss the barriers that currently impede this process and potential strategies for overcoming them. The information presented here is based on the background study of the literature, interviews with key stakeholders, and focus groups with parents in at-risk communities in Allegheny County.

Screening Requirements and Recommendations

Federal Requirements and Recommendations

According to the 1998 Medicaid Manual, a lead screening test must be provided at the ages of 12 and 24 months to all children enrolled in Medicaid. A child between 36 and 72 months of age who has not received a prior blood lead test must be screened. No risk assessment is required.

The Health Resources and Services Administration (HRSA) within HHS provides grants for health services in medically underserved areas and establishes federal policies for children receiving these services. The 1994 HRSA Bureau of Primary Health Care Policy for Health Centers calls for an assessment of risk for lead poisoning at each well-child visit and other pediatric visits, as appropriate, for children between the ages of six months and six years. Children assessed at high risk for lead poisoning must be screened at six months or when first determined to be at high risk. Children assessed at low risk for lead poisoning must receive an initial lead screen at age 12 months. We note that the HRSA guidelines are not consistent with federal Medicaid requirements, reflecting the view that the dangers of lead toxicity do not end at 24 months of age.

For all other children, the CDC's blood lead screening recommendations should be followed, unless superseded by specific state or county recommendations. The CDC's most recent (November 1997) guidelines call for universal screening of children at 12 and 24 months of age (and of those between the ages of 36 and 72 months who have not been previously tested) in communities with inadequate data on the prevalence of elevated blood lead levels, and in communities in which 27 percent or more of the dwellings were built before 1950. Targeted screening is recommended in communities where less than 12 percent of children have blood lead levels of 10 µg/dL or greater, or where less than 27 percent of dwellings were built before 1950. The CDC further recommends that state and local health officials develop statewide plans for childhood blood lead screening and better target children who are at specific risk.

In general, there is ongoing debate within the public health policy community regarding the appropriate ages for screening. Some experts recommend that pregnant women and those who are likely to become pregnant should be screened for elevated blood lead levels and that all newborns should be routinely tested for lead at birth. These recommendations are based on recent research indicating that the vulnerabilities of a child's nervous system to lead poisoning are greatest during their earliest years, as discussed in Chapter One.

State and Local Recommendations

As stated previously, the PA DOH's Lead Elimination Plan calls for universal screening of all children at one and two years of age, and for all children three to six years old without a confirmed prior lead blood test (PA DOH, 2005). The ACHD endorses the PA DOH's call for universal screening of all children at ages one and two years.

Risk Assessment and Lead Screening Processes in Allegheny County

Figure 3.1 illustrates the processes of risk assessment and lead screening for young children as these currently occur in Allegheny County. When a young child is taken to a health care provider for a wellness checkup at nine to 12 months of age and again at 24 months of age, his or her risk for lead poisoning should be assessed. Those at risk have their blood drawn and tested for elevated blood lead levels.

Figure 3.1
Risk Assessment and Screening Processes for Children in Allegheny County

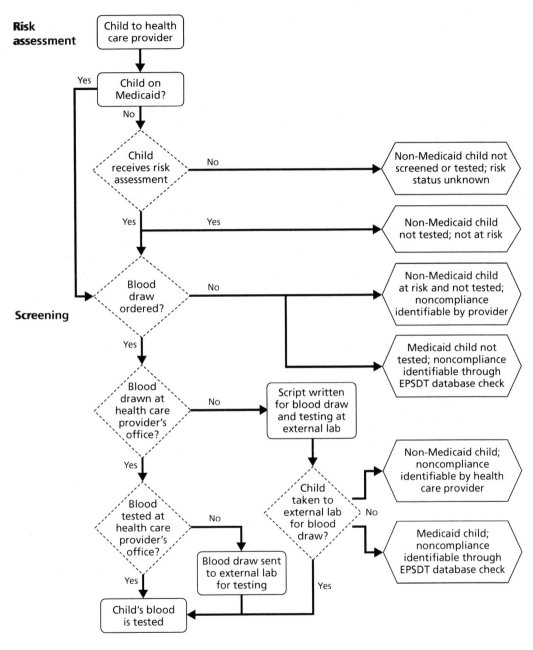

Visit to a Health Care Provider

For regular well-child checkups, most children are taken to a pediatrician, family doctor, or neighborhood health center, but some might also encounter a health care provider in other settings (e.g., WIC offices, Head Start programs, or community health fairs). Immunization data from the CDC indicate that most young children nationwide are receiving medical care in their early years and thus are being seen by health care providers who could assess their risk for lead poisoning and screen them, as appropriate (CDC, National Center for Health Statistics, 2003).[1]

In Allegheny County, blood lead screening tests are covered under Medicaid, the State Children's Health Insurance Program (SCHIP),[2] and some private health plans. Unlike Medicaid, however, SCHIP and private health plans merely pay for lead screening services; they do not mandate them. In 2000, of Allegheny County's 71,081 children under the age of six, approximately 27,844 (39 percent) were privately insured; 25,195 (35 percent) were covered under Medicaid; 12,853 (18 percent) were covered under SCHIP; and 5,189 (7 percent) were uninsured.[3] The PA DPW has established the HealthChoices Program to provide physical health and behavioral health care services for those receiving Medicaid through four MCOs in Allegheny County. Three of these are physical health MCOs, providing primary care and other medical services, including screening for childhood lead poisoning.

Risk Assessment

Risk assessment questionnaires have typically been used to assess a non-Medicaid child's risk for lead poisoning (i.e., all Medicaid children are considered at risk and must be screened). The CDC guidelines recommend that this risk assessment be conducted at between nine and 12 months of age and, if possible, again at 24 months of age. The CDC further recommends that the risk assessment questionnaire include at least three questions:

---

[1] According to a random sample of telephone interviews conducted in 2003, supplemented by a survey of immunization providers for the interview participants, 94 percent of all children 19 to 35 months of age, and 83 percent of those classified as below the poverty level, had received at least one of the eight recommended vaccines. Eighty-one percent of all children 19 to 35 months of age, and 76 percent of those classified as below the poverty level, had received the combined series of eight vaccines.

[2] SCHIP, administered by the Centers for Medicare and Medicaid Services (CMS), is a state-administered program for expanding health insurance coverage to children whose families earn too much for traditional Medicaid, yet not enough to afford private health insurance. Each state sets its own guidelines regarding eligibility and services.

[3] The most recent data for the state of Pennsylvania as a whole show that 4 percent of children under 17 years old in Pennsylvania are uninsured; 29 percent have public coverage; 70 percent are covered by private insurance; and 1 percent are covered through the military. Of those children in Pennsylvania who are uninsured, 19 percent are under five years old; 14 percent are between six to ten years old; and 68 percent are 11 to 18 years old (PA DOI, 2005).

1. Does your child live in or regularly visit a house that was built before 1950?
2. Does your child live in or regularly visit a house built before 1978 with recent (within the last six months) or ongoing renovations or remodeling?
3. Does your child have a sibling or playmate who has or did have lead poisoning?

Health care providers may also ask whether the child's parent or caregiver has an occupation or hobby that exposes him or her to high levels of lead (e.g., lead soldering, pottery making, furniture refinishing) or about other circumstances they believe indicate a risk factor for lead poisoning in their communities.

A child who is administered this questionnaire and found not to be at risk requires no follow-up unless conditions change (i.e., the family moves or renovates their house, the child spends time in a place that may introduce lead hazards, or a sibling is found to have lead poisoning). Under current federal guidelines, this child has been successfully assessed as not being at risk for lead poisoning and the health care provider is entirely in compliance.

A child who is not administered this questionnaire and not screened for lead poisoning may be at risk but not identified. Unless a parent, day care provider, or someone else actively manages that child's assessment for lead, it will never be known whether that child is at risk for lead poisoning or has an elevated blood lead level.

Note that at present in Allegheny County, there is no way of knowing if a risk assessment has or has not been conducted for a non-Medicaid child. However, if the PA DOH's recommendation for universal screening is adopted and successfully implemented, all children 12 and 24 months old in Allegheny County should be screened for lead poisoning, thereby obviating the need for a risk assessment questionnaire altogether.

Lead Screening Test

If a child is on Medicaid or found to be at risk through the risk assessment questionnaire, the child's blood should be drawn and tested. The health care provider may conduct this screening test in his or her office, or write a prescription for the parent to take the child to an off-site laboratory for blood lead screening.

An initial lead screen in a health care provider's office or at an off-site laboratory can be administered through the use of venous or capillary (fingerstick) blood lead tests. The CDC recommends venous collection as the most accurate method of blood lead testing. However, with good collection protocol, capillary testing is also acceptable as an initial screening method. Capillary collection may be subject to contamination by surface lead on the finger, the likelihood of which is decreased with proper technique (Schlenker et al., 1994). One study has found that a capillary value of 10 µg/dL or higher has a 91-percent sensitivity for venous lead values of 10 µg/dL or higher (Sargent and Dalton, 1996). The CDC has published a recommended collection protocol that should decrease the possibility of specimen contamination. Filter-paper technology has been accurate when proper collection technique is utilized.

After a child's blood is drawn, either in a health care provider's office or a laboratory, it is tested. Under PA DOH regulations, laboratories analyzing blood lead tests conducted in Pennsylvania are required to be approved and licensed as clinical laboratories. Laboratories are reimbursed differently for blood lead specimen collection and analysis, depending on how the child is insured. Some health insurance companies reimburse laboratories on a fee-for-service basis; others use capitated rates (i.e., bundled payments for a number of services provided).

When sending a blood lead sample to a laboratory, the health care provider should include enough information about the patient so that the laboratory can adequately report the results back to the office and to the state via PA-NEDSS. If the child's blood is drawn at the lab, the patient information comes directly from the parent.

For Medicaid children, a blood lead test result equal to or greater than 10 µg/dL obtained by capillary specimen must be confirmed using a venous blood sample. CDC guidelines recommend the same for all other children. The PA DPW has communicated this requirement to all medical assistance providers.

Barriers to Lead Screening in Allegheny County and Potential Strategies for Overcoming Them

Although national surveys of pediatricians indicate that they know the requirements and recommendations for childhood lead screening, available data at the national, state, and local levels suggest that these guidelines are often not followed. The U.S. GAO has identified several possible explanations for this, including the failure of federal and state agencies to monitor or ensure the implementation of blood lead screening policies; varying perceptions of the seriousness of the problem; and general difficulties in providing preventive care to the Medicaid population (GAO, 1999).

A 1995 AAP survey of 734 primary care pediatricians found that 53 percent of pediatricians attempt to screen all of their patients up to 36 months of age with a blood test for lead toxicity; 38 percent attempt to screen some of their patients; and 9 percent screen none of their patients in this age group (AAP, Division of Health Policy Research, 1995). Ninety percent of pediatricians who do not universally screen their patients (including those who do not screen any of their patients) up to 36 months of age say they do not do so because of the low prevalence of venous lead levels 10 µg/dL or greater among their patients. About one-third of pediatricians who selectively screen for lead poisoning say lead screening is too costly (33 percent) and that other issues are more important to review with parents (34 percent). On the other hand, 59 percent of surveyed pediatricians believe interventions for children nine to 36 months of age who have blood lead levels between 10 and 19 µg/dL are effective in reducing lead levels.

Perceptions of the Importance of Lead Screening

The dramatic reduction in extremely high blood lead levels in young children has reinforced the general perception that childhood lead poisoning is no longer a public health concern and that screening is not important for young children.

Interviews with local public health officials and health care providers in Allegheny County suggest that lead poisoning is not typically viewed as an urgent public health priority, particularly relative to other childhood medical issues, such as asthma, obesity, and depression. The extent to which these professionals are aware of the emerging literature regarding the developmental neurotoxicity of lead even at relatively low levels remains unclear. Certain groups of local parents, on the other hand, appear to be knowledgeable about the potential impact of lead poisoning on their children and the importance of lead screening.

Public perceptions about the importance of childhood blood lead screening can be informed by disseminating to health care providers and parents information regarding lead screening requirements and recommendations, and data that justify them at the local level. A number of innovative and effective health promotion and education strategies have been implemented by a number of states. Rhode Island's *Lead Screening Plan* offers some useful examples of these (Rhode Island Department of Health, Childhood Lead Poisoning Prevention Program, 2000):

- **Lead Month.** Each May, representatives from community-based organizations, health and child care providers, and other state and local government groups organize community-level activities to help promote the prevention of childhood lead poisoning. A calendar of activities is developed and distributed statewide.
- **Outreach to Providers.** Staff from the state's Childhood Lead Poisoning Prevention Program periodically visit the offices of pediatricians and family practitioners to offer technical assistance (i.e., screening guidelines and case management information) and distribute promotional items, posters, and educational brochures.
- **Media Campaign.** An integrated media campaign, under the theme "Lead Poisoning: Danger in Every Corner," is conducted annually through a variety of communication channels (e.g., bus cards, television and radio public service announcements and/or guest appearances, distribution of posters and brochures through mailings and direct outreach, and other grassroots activities).
- **"Keep It Clean" Campaign.** Dedicated to eliminating lead poisoning through consumer education on lead-safety guidelines for work in the home, the core of

this campaign is a set of partnerships with local hardware and paint stores, where families already go to receive "how-to" information and to purchase materials. The campaign also includes press releases and articles in the media.

- **Parent Consultant.** A parent consultant works with the state's CLPPP staff, serving as a liaison to parents and participating in community presentations, outreach, and peer education.
- **"Lead Update."** This bimonthly publication is distributed by fax and mail to pediatricians and family practitioners, community-based agencies, child and health care providers, and schools. It contains the latest information on the Rhode Island CLPPP's new efforts, research findings, policies, statistics, quality assurance efforts, upcoming events, and other field-related issues.
- **Web Page.** The Rhode Island CLPPP's Web page is updated continuously and contains the last three to four years of lead poisoning data, past editions of the "Lead Update," as well as the Program's rules and regulations. It also offers a way to get educational brochures, contact the staff, and link to other related sites.
- **Educational Materials.** A variety of educational materials are available to parents, professionals, and health care providers, including information about prevention measures, the importance of nutrition for children and pregnant women, the sources of lead poisoning, and ways to prevent exposure, among others.
- **Toll-Free Line.** A toll-free line (with bilingual English and Spanish capability) is available Monday through Friday to respond to consumers' questions about lead poisoning, provide referrals to other services, and serve as the Rhode Island Department of Health's first friendly point of contact with the public.

Targeted Screening

Federal screening requirements and state and local screening recommendations notwithstanding, many health care providers may be continuing to follow a policy of targeted screening (e.g., use of a risk assessment questionnaire to determine the need to screen non-Medicaid children), which adds several decision points to the determination that a child is at risk for lead poisoning. At each of these decision points, some at-risk children may not be identified and therefore not screened.

Several local stakeholders believe that the effect of targeted screening via a risk assessment questionnaire has been to lower the screening rate for truly at-risk children in Allegheny County. Although complete and accurate data are unavailable at this time, we do know that, overall, fewer children are being screened in Allegheny County than 15 years ago, and there is a noticeable reduction in screening at age 24 months.

There is also a chance that the health care provider will not administer the risk assessment questionnaire at all. The 1995 AAP survey found that 41 percent of pediatricians who screen for lead poisoning use a risk assessment questionnaire to identify young children at risk for lead poisoning (AAP, Division of Health Policy Research, 1995). We do not know how many children who have not been screened for lead poisoning have also not been assessed for risk of lead poisoning.

The practice of targeting resources to at-risk populations appears to be ineffective in other areas of health care as well. For example, according to one advisory group member, when flu shots were to be administered only to certain high-risk groups of children, an estimated 10 percent of those at risk actually received the shots. The guidelines were subsequently changed, mandating flu shots for all children between six and 23 months old, thus enabling health care providers to administer flu shots in a more comprehensive and cost-efficient manner.

With respect to lead screening in particular, screening rates are highest where states have their own statutes or regulations with specific screening requirements (GAO, 1999). Effective implementation of the PA DOH's recommendation for universal screening will obviate the need for targeted screening and therefore resolve many of the barriers associated with the risk assessment process.

Conducting a Screening Test

Among those interviewed and in the literature, there are reported concerns about drawing blood from young children, the appropriateness of capillary samples, and the skills of the staff collecting the samples. Venous draws can be difficult to perform on very young children, increasing the reluctance of many health care providers to use this procedure. Capillary draws, though easier to perform, pose issues for some practitioners regarding the validity of the results, as there is risk of either contamination (the finger is not wiped clean enough and lead on the finger contaminates the blood sample) or coagulation. When the blood is collected into a tube, if the blood coagulates before it is tested, the sample cannot be analyzed. Coagulation is not a concern with samples collected on filter paper.

The issue of venous versus capillary sampling procedures is important because the rate of completed blood lead screenings increases when screenings are conducted in health care providers' offices. In most cases, this means that a capillary sample is taken by the health care provider and then sent to a licensed laboratory for analysis and reporting.

Taking into account numerous studies that support the validity of capillary samples, one local Medicaid physical health MCO has strongly encouraged the use of capillary draws in health care providers' offices in conjunction with filter-paper techniques. Another local MCO significantly increased its EPSDT-compliance rate by contracting with a laboratory that provides collection materials for health care providers to use in their offices. This initiative also dramatically increased the information that the MCO had on the blood lead levels of its members.

Screening Referrals

Because many health care providers prefer to have lead screening tests conducted through venous blood draws and do not have readily available pediatric blood-drawers, many children are referred to off-site laboratories for testing. This action requires a number of additional steps by the parent or guardian, including identifying and finding the laboratory, arranging for transportation to get there, taking time off from work, finding child care for any other children who must remain at home, among others.

As there is a noticeable decline in the rate of blood lead specimens obtained when the lead screening test is not conducted in the health care provider's office, and this is true across socioeconomic groups (Vivier et al., 2001), strategies for facilitating lead screening in health care providers' offices are key to overcoming the barriers associated with referring a child for a blood screen at an off-site laboratory.

CHAPTER FOUR

Reporting and Surveillance of Childhood Lead Poisoning in Allegheny County

Reporting the results of childhood blood lead screens is essential for two reasons: It expedites the case management and treatment of an individual child with an elevated blood lead level, and it provides the data necessary to characterize the epidemiology of elevated blood lead levels (PA DOH, 2005). The latter is particularly important because the prevalence of elevated blood lead levels can vary even within a community. Complete and accurate surveillance information about local lead poisoning risk factors can help guide development of appropriate screening recommendations, reinforce public education efforts regarding the importance of childhood screening, and encourage strategic partnerships for improving primary prevention efforts as well as screening and reporting.

In this chapter, we present current blood lead reporting requirements, describe the reporting and surveillance processes as they occur in Allegheny County, and discuss the barriers that currently impede these processes, along with potential strategies for overcoming them. The information presented here is based on the findings of the background study of the literature and interviews with key state and local stakeholders, particularly those involved with the blood lead level reporting and surveillance processes.

National and State Reporting Requirements for Blood Lead Screening

HCFA, which administers Medicaid, requires each state to report the number of blood lead tests that are given each year (Form HCFA-416). Most states and jurisdictions have laboratory-reporting requirements to ensure that blood lead results are reported. However, not all require the reporting of all (elevated and nonelevated) blood lead test results.

In Pennsylvania, laboratories are required to report results of all blood lead tests on both venous and capillary specimens for persons under 16 years of age (and venous blood levels of 25 µg/dL or higher in persons 16 years of age or older) to the PA DOH. Laboratories must report this data electronically using PA-NEDSS. Health care providers and health care facilities are required to report level results of all cases they treat for lead poisoning (i.e., a lead level of 20 µg/dL or higher, or two or more venous blood lead levels of 15 to 19 µg/dL [inclusive] from samples drawn three months apart), for persons under 16 years of age, and for pregnant women. Mandatory patient information includes name, sex, date of birth, telephone number, and street address (or zip code of the ordering provider's address, or zip code of the address of the facility where the specimen was drawn, if the patient's address is unknown). Mandatory lead test information includes the date of specimen collection; the name of the test; the type of specimen collection used (venous or capillary); the date the analysis was performed; the test result; the range of normal values for the test; and the name, address, and telephone number of the health care provider for whom the test was performed.

Reporting and Surveillance Processes in Allegheny County

Figure 4.1 illustrates the processes of childhood blood lead level reporting and surveillance as they currently occur in Allegheny County. Once a child's blood specimen has been tested (i.e., through the processes described in Chapter Three), laboratories send the results to the health care provider who ordered the test; PA-NEDSS; and, if the laboratory is reimbursed by the patient's insurance company on a fee-for-service basis, to the insurance company responsible for the child. Each entity to which the results are sent requests different information and uses that information differently.

Reporting to Health Care Providers

Laboratories send the results to the health care provider who ordered the test so he or she can take appropriate action if needed. When children are given a prescription for a blood screening test but do not obtain the test, there is no feedback mechanism for informing the health care provider that the test was not conducted. Some providers may later discover the lack of a blood screening test result in the child's medical record, but there is no guarantee of this.

In the case of a child on Medicaid, the MCO might notify the health care provider that the child has not received a lead screening, but if the provider has sent in a claim indicating that an EPSDT screening was completed, identifying the lack of a blood lead screening test is not likely.

Figure 4.1
Blood Level Reporting and Surveillance Processes in Allegheny County

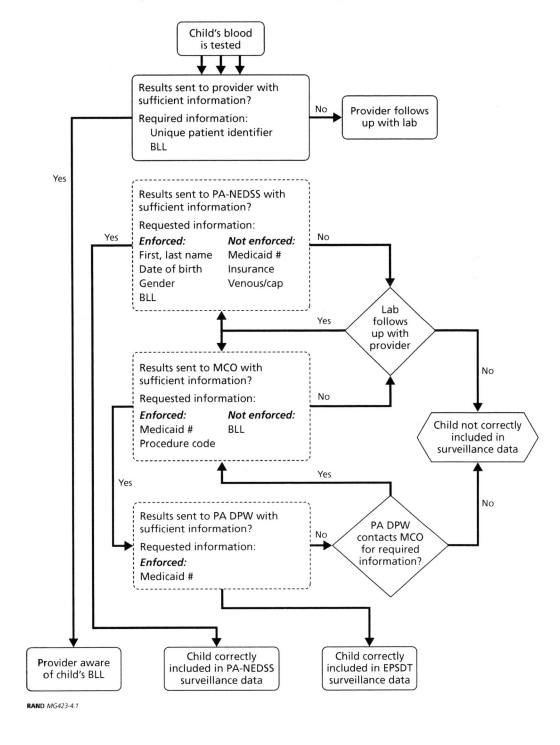

Reporting to PA-NEDSS

The interviews conducted for this study and written documentation for PA-NEDSS suggest that the design and reporting elements that PA DOH regulations require for PA-NEDSS are sufficient to provide for a complete surveillance system for all children, including at-risk children and children on Medicaid. However, at present, blood lead results will be accepted by PA-NEDSS with a subset of the data elements required by regulation. Medicaid status information is not required for specimen results to be entered into PA-NEDSS.

The data reported to PA-NEDSS are used to identify children with elevated blood lead levels and to ensure that appropriate case management, medical interventions, or environmental investigations are conducted.

The PA DOH follows up on any apparent data integrity problems with an individual specimen with the laboratory reporting the data or a CLPPP.

Reporting to and by Insurers and MCOs

For billing purposes, if the laboratory is paid on a fee-for-service basis for lead screens conducted or samples tested, it will send the claim information to the insurer. On their own initiative, some large local laboratories also send the blood lead level data to a child's Medicaid MCO.

In the case of Medicaid, claims data for clients who are enrolled in an MCO provide the basis for identifying which children have been screened. MCOs report to the providers in their networks on the individual Medicaid children who do not have completed EPSDT screens. The MCOs have a record of each child and his or her health care provider. This is an advantage that PA DOH does not have in measuring compliance with screening recommendations and requirements. However, because blood lead levels are generally not reported to Medicaid MCOs, identifying children with elevated blood lead levels is the responsibility of the health care provider. Once identified, the MCO's Special Needs Coordinator is available to assist with follow-up.

Reporting to and by PA DPW

Local MCOs regularly report the number of EPSDT screenings conducted to the PA DPW. However, in the interest of minimizing reporting requirements of MCOs, the PA DPW recently ceased collecting blood lead levels for young Medicaid children who are screened. Thus, the PA DPW no longer knows the rate of elevated blood lead levels among Pennsylvania residents, and neither do the MCOs. The PA DPW reports to CMS the number and rate of EPSDT screenings completed each year; blood lead levels are not reported.

Barriers to Reporting and Surveillance in Allegheny County and Potential Strategies for Overcoming Them

A range of issues related to childhood blood lead level data transmission, completeness, quality assurance, and feedback currently impede reporting and surveillance processes in Allegheny County, particularly with respect to PA-NEDSS and Medicaid data.

Data Transmission

Representatives of some state-licensed blood lead laboratories that serve health care providers in Allegheny County reported difficulties with regard to reporting electronically to PA-NEDSS. For example, an interviewee from one large local laboratory stated that it was difficult to provide blood lead data in the HL7 format specified by the PA DOH for reporting to PA-NEDSS, given the large number of screens the laboratory reports each week. Others noted that in smaller laboratories, limited staffing and inadequate computer knowledge of current staff continue to hamper efforts to meet the electronic reporting requirements of PA-NEDSS. Additional technical assistance from the PA-DOH for those laboratories having difficulty reporting to PA-NEDSS appears warranted.

Completeness of Data

Many of the professionals involved in surveillance systems and at local laboratories reported that health care providers are "notorious" for providing incomplete patient and/or lead test information on specimens sent for external processing and reporting. Some laboratories will follow up with providers to obtain the required information; others will report to PA-NEDSS only the information they are provided.

Since only a few of the data fields required by regulation must actually be completed when submitting a report to PA-NEDSS, the data available are very often incomplete, making it difficult to identify the child for case management or to use the information for surveillance. In particular, the lack of Medicaid-status information on blood lead specimen results entered into PA-NEDSS makes it impossible to reliably cross-reference PA-NEDSS data with Medicaid data. Since the PA DPW no longer collects blood lead levels of young children when they are screened, it can be difficult to identify those children who require follow-up.

Among the three physical health MCOs serving Allegheny County, there are different reporting issues that make it difficult for the MCOs to know with certainty the rate at which children's blood lead levels are being screened or prescribed for screening. The challenges vary with the policies and procedures of the respective MCOs. Some health care providers do not always utilize the EPSDT codes available to them. Some MCO reporting systems have a procedure code for EPSDT screening but do not require additional codes for individual screens. Laboratory procedures may be funded by a capitated rate, and thus, claims data on individual children may not be available.

Absent reliable data on the prevalence of elevated blood lead levels, screening for lead poisoning becomes just one more reporting requirement that does not necessarily result in coordinated efforts to resolve the problems or enable public officials to know if a problem has been solved. To bridge this gap between reporting and problem solving, many interviewees suggested more stringent enforcement of current PA-NEDSS reporting requirements. They believe that the current lack of enforcement has yielded invalid, unreliable data and significant underreporting of screenings that have actually been conducted. With regard to Medicaid in particular, reinstituting the requirement for reporting blood lead levels would assist in problem solving for children who have been identified as having elevated blood lead levels and for the specific communities in which they reside.

Quality Assurance

Until recently, there have been very few staff within the PA DOH assigned to monitor blood lead level data and identify data integrity problems. The approach of the PA DOH has been to hold the laboratory responsible for complete information, but laboratory-licensing procedures do not include adequate review of adherence to reporting requirements for blood lead level screening.

Feedback Mechanisms

Although the interviews conducted for this study did not identify any local difficulties with health care providers receiving blood lead specimen results from laboratories if the parent took the child to be screened, a recent study of screening outcomes in Michigan found that half of Medicaid-enrolled children with elevated blood lead levels have no follow-up testing, and those children at greatest risk of having elevated blood lead levels are less likely to receive follow-up (Kemper et al, 2005).

The local Medicaid MCOs interviewed indicated that, historically, the PA DPW OMAP has not aggressively monitored blood lead screening rates. However, since lead screening is one element of the accreditation process for Medicaid MCOs, standardized measures and public reporting of the results can motivate them to develop strategies for improving blood lead screening rates.

Recently, the OMAP has established performance measurements for the HealthChoices MCOs regarding the number of children who have had a blood lead level screen. Medicaid data could also be used to create report cards for MCOs to identify the extent to which EPSDT requirements are fulfilled. Based on the experiences of other communities with high compliance rates for blood lead screening, if health care providers receive a report card comparing their screening rates to those of other providers in their network, more Medicaid children will be screened. To date, at least one MCO in Allegheny County that reported network-wide provider performance on blood lead screening received additional requests from individual providers asking for their practice-specific data.

A best-practice initiative for improving childhood blood lead screening in Rhode Island has demonstrated that effective partnerships between the Rhode Island Department of Health and local MCOs and health care providers can improve screening (HHS, 2002). In November 2000, Rhode Island's three local Medicaid MCOs and Department of Health formed a partnership designed to facilitate sharing of childhood blood lead level data. A workgroup was formed consisting of representatives from the Rhode Island Department of Health CLPPP and the MCOs. The mutual goals were to improve the ability to determine which children have been screened and to formulate strategies to screen the remaining children who were eligible for screening but were not tested.

The initiative had several core components: (1) on a quarterly basis, children enrolled in participating MCOs who were 24 to 26 months old and had no claim records for a lead screening were identified; (2) the list of children without a screening claim was provided to the Department of Health and electronically matched against its lead poisoning surveillance database; (3) a list of children who also had no screening record in the surveillance database was returned to the accountable MCO, which then contacted each child's health care provider and asked if the child had been screened, if the office would follow up, or if additional interventions were needed; (4) when the children were 28 to 30 months old, a final data comparison was made to identify all additional children who had been screened as a result of this intervention.

The Rhode Island CLPPP provided technical assistance in the form of project oversight, data management and analysis, and report generation. MCOs received lists of unscreened children, performed a comparison against their records, forwarded the information to primary care providers for assessment and intervention, and reported outcomes to the CLPPP.

Prior to the statewide collaborative intervention in Rhode Island in November 2000, 82.5 percent of children were screened for lead poisoning by 30 months of age. Seven months later, the lead poisoning screening rate for children 30 months of age or younger was 87 percent.

Follow up for non-Medicaid children referred for blood lead screens who are not tested is more complicated, since there is no ready mechanism for others outside the provider's office to identify them. In this case, health care providers should be encouraged to develop an internal tracking ("tickler") system for identifying individual children in their practices for whom a blood draw was ordered but whose blood was not tested.

CHAPTER FIVE

Conclusions and Recommendations

The findings of this study suggest that current blood lead level reporting and surveillance data are inadequate to accurately assess the true prevalence of childhood lead poisoning in Allegheny County or the number of children who are at risk for lead poisoning but have not yet been screened. At the same time, estimates based on the existing data indicate the need for more diligent state and local involvement to ensure that at-risk children in Allegheny County are screened and that the information is reported properly. Ideally, this information should be integrated into one database so that prevalence rates and children at risk for lead poisoning who have not been screened can be identified and appropriate action taken.

In this chapter, we offer a set of overall state-level recommendations for improving screening, reporting, and surveillance in Allegheny County. We have organized these recommendations into long- and near-term actions that should be coordinated through the leadership of public entities that have a mandate to address these issues, including the PA DOH, the PA DPW, the Pennsylvania Department of Insurance (PA DOI),[1] the ACHD, and the Medicaid MCOs serving Allegheny County. In addition, we present a set of specific recommendations for overcoming barriers with regard to screening, reporting, and surveillance in Allegheny County to be implemented under the leadership of the ACHD in collaboration with the appropriate state entities. While we recognize the ongoing policy debates regarding the appropriate ages for screening and the minimally acceptable threshold for elevated blood lead levels, the recommendations presented here reflect the current consensus of the CDC and other federal and state entities responsible for childhood lead poisoning.

---

[1] The Pennsylvania Department of Insurance is responsible for administering the laws of the Commonwealth as they pertain to the regulation of the insurance industry and the protection of the insurance consumer.

Overall Recommendations

Long-Term Recommendations

The findings of this study confirm that universal childhood blood lead level screening is indicated for Allegheny County, according to CDC criteria. Therefore, we support the implementation of the PA DOH Lead Elimination Plan's recommendation to institute universal blood lead screening for *all* children at one and two years of age. Proactive implementation of universal screening by counties that meet CDC criteria should, by definition, work to ameliorate the racial disparities in blood lead level data that are currently evident at the national level.

We also recommend that the PA DPW Office of Child Development and the PA DOH request that the PA DOI adopt the Medicaid blood lead screening requirements for children who are beneficiaries of the SCHIP program.

After the collection of more complete and accurate data over the next few years, it may be possible to move to a targeted screening approach. Such an approach will be facilitated by the use of one integrated database for surveillance of childhood blood lead levels in Pennsylvania. We recommend that the PA DOH and PA DPW use PA-NEDSS for this purpose.

Near-Term Recommendations

We recommend that the PA DOH enforce current PA-NESSS blood lead reporting requirements, including standards of reporting that must be met by all state-licensed laboratories. At a minimum, the PA DOH should require that the provision of information on children's insurance include Medicaid identification.

We also recommend that the PA DOH provide more extensive technical assistance and support to state-licensed blood lead laboratories on proper electronic reporting. We recommend that the PA DPW reinstitute the requirements for reporting blood lead levels for all Medicaid children who are screened, or explore other options for obtaining this information, such as utilizing PA-NEDSS data.

We also recommend that the PA DPW OMAP step up its efforts to aggressively monitor current EPSDT requirements for childhood blood lead level screening, establishing a goal of 90-percent compliance for MCOs in Allegheny County by 2006. Managed care contracts should be revised to include quality or performance standards relating specifically to lead.

Finally, we recommend that the PA DOH and the PA DPW establish procedures for cross-referencing blood lead level surveillance data in the PA-NEDSS and Medicaid databases no later than July 2006. This collaboration should be extended to joint efforts with the ACHD, local MCOs, and laboratories in order to utilize local blood lead level information to the fullest extent possible.

Additional Recommendations for Improving Screening in Allegheny County

We recommend that the ACHD, the Medicaid MCOs serving Allegheny County, and interested local organizations enhance public education of parents and health care providers about the importance of repeat blood lead level screening at age two and the adverse effects of elevated blood lead levels of 10 µg/dL or higher on early childhood neurodevelopment. Specifically, we recommend that the ACHD and the Medicaid MCOs serving Allegheny County add this information to their educational materials for parents and their periodic updates to participating practices, that the ACHD accelerate involvement of other community agencies and organizations serving young children in this public education campaign, and that the Pennsylvania Chapter of the AAP include this information in its newsletters to health care providers. Particular attention should be paid to ensuring that all educational materials are culturally appropriate for different racial and ethnic groups.

To increase the rate of blood lead screening in health care providers' offices, we also recommend educating health care providers on the validity of capillary draws. The PA DPW, the ACHD, and Medicaid MCOs should assume responsibility for ensuring that health care providers are supplied with training and kits for in-house capillary-specimen collection (including filter paper) and export of specimens to licensed blood lead laboratories for all Medicaid children; the ACHD and the PA DOH should strongly encourage the adoption by private commercial insurers of the same practices for all other children. We further recommend that the Pennsylvania Chapter of the AAP add blood lead screening tests to the immunization record they provide for distribution to parents.

To better address the issue of potential neurodevelopmental delays resulting from relatively low blood lead levels in children, we recommend that the ACHD establish a two- to three-year pilot program with the Alliance for Infants and Toddlers (Alliance) for developmental screening and tracking of a sample of children with blood lead levels of 10 µg/dL or higher, thus offering these children the benefits of the developmental screening and tracking process already conducted by the Alliance. Based on these data, state and local policymakers could assess the extent to which developmental delays are identified in this population at a significant rate. Additional partners in this initiative should include the ACHD (to determine if this program should be incorporated into the its portfolio of prevention efforts), the PA DPW Office of Child Development, and the PA DOH Maternal and Child Health Program.

Additional Recommendations for Improving Reporting and Surveillance in Allegheny County

We recommend that all Medicaid MCOs serving Allegheny County send feedback reports to their network providers on individual Medicaid children not screened for lead poisoning, including comparative data on blood lead screening compliance rates across practices. For all other children, the ACHD and SCHIP administrators should encourage health care providers to develop an internal tracking ("tickler") system for identifying individual children for whom a blood draw was ordered by an external lab but whose blood was not tested.

Population of Children and Median Housing Age in Allegheny County

Table A.1
Number of Children in Allegheny County Under Age Five Living in Census Tracts Where Median-Age Housing Was Built Before 1950, as of 2000

Census Tract	Median Year Structure Built	Neighborhood/Municipality	Number of Children Under 5 Years Old
2201	1940	Allegheny West	23
1803	1940	Allentown	210
1603	1940	Arlington	114
1604	1940	Arlington Heights	41
4230	1940	Aspinwall	162
4323, 4324	1940–1948	Avalon Borough	268
509	1944	Bedford Dwellings	292
1916, 1920	1940-1942	Beechview	476
4311, 4314, 4315	1940–1942	Bellevue Borough	434
1809	1940	Beltzhoover	170
4340	1940	Ben Avon Borough	145
4330	1940	Ben Avon Heights	33
802	1940	Bloomfield	361
103	1940	Bluff	42
1806	1947	Bon Air	42
4020	1940	Brackenridge	171
5138	1940	Braddock Borough	209
4781, 4782	1945–1947	Brentwood Borough	557

Table A.1—Continued

Census Tract	Median Year Structure Built	Neighborhood/Municipality	Number of Children Under 5 Years Old
2701	1940	Brighton Heights	466
1917, 1918, 1919	1940–1948	Brookline	678
2507	1940	California-Kirkbride	84
4687, 4688	1940	Carnegie Borough (2 of 3)	238
2901	1940	Carrick	571
901	1940	Central Lawrenceville	208
2206	1940	Central North Side	145
405	1942	Central Oakland	82
5110	1944	Chalfant Borough	42
4927, 4928, 4929	1940–1945	Clairton City (3 of 4)	316
4507, 4508	1940–1942	Coraopolis Borough	336
2815	1940	Crafton Heights	103
4722	1940	Dormont Borough	496
4870	1943	Dravosburg Borough	117
4868, 4869	1940–1945	Duquesne City (2 of 3)	354
1911	1944	Duquesne Heights	93
2304	1940	East Allegheny	102
2805	1940	East Carnegie	22
4040	1940	East Deer Township	84
1113	1940	East Liberty	201
5070	1940	East McKeesport Borough	130
5100	1940	East Pittsburgh Borough	148
5161	1940	Edgewood Borough	166
4460	1940	Edgeworth Borough	125
4940	1940	Elizabeth Borough	86
2020	1940	Elliot	179
2017	1940	Esplen	35
4250	1940	Etna	207
2808	1948	Fairywood	145

Table A.1—Continued

Census Tract	Median Year Structure Built	Neighborhood/Municipality	Number of Children Under 5 Years Old
2509	1940	Fineview	208
807	1940	Friendship	65
1016, 1017	1940–1944	Garfield	461
4993	1941–1946	Glassport Borough	229
4420	1940	Glenfield Borough	12
1516, 1517	1940–1941	Greenfield	350
4011, 4012, 4013	1940–1949	Harrison Township	617
3101	1940	Hays	23
4430	1940	Haysville Borough	2
1501	1940	Hazelwood	308
4710	1940	Heidelberg Borough	62
2406	1940	Herr's Island	141
1102	1940	Highland Park	373
4838	1940	Homestead Borough	210
1301, 1302	1940–1942	Homewood North	339
1303, 1304	1943–1944	Homewood South	288
1207	1940	Homewood West	61
4643	1940	Ingram Borough	205
4360	1948	Kilbuck Township	38
3001	1940	Knoxville	317
1204	1940	Larimer	75
4480	1940	Leetsdale Borough	63
1201, 1202, 1203	1940–1946	Lincoln-Lemington-Belmar	253
603	1940	Lower Lawrenceville	150
2107	1940	Manchester	185
2704	1940	Marshall-Shadeland	323
4540	1940	McDonald Borough	124
4639	1940	McKees Rocks Borough	437

Table A.1—Continued

Census Tract	Median Year Structure Built	Neighborhood/Municipality	Number of Children Under 5 Years Old
5509, 5512, 5520, 5521, 5522, 5523, 5524	1940–1946	McKeesport City (7 out of 9)	1,191
501	1946	Middle Hill	79
4270	1940	Millvale	252
1014	1940	Morningside	185
4731, 4732, 4734.01, 4735	1941–1947	Mount Lebanon (4 of 8)	931
4810	1940	Mount Oliver Borough	242
1807	1940	Mount Washington	482
1607	1940	Mount Oliver	33
4843, 4845, 4846	1940–1948	Munhall Borough	646
4610	1948	Neville Township	66
5120	1940	North Braddock Borough	396
403, 404	1940–1944	North Oakland	39
4550	1946	Oakdale Borough	74
5252, 5253	1945–1947	Oakmont Borough (2 of 3)	203
4440	1944	Osborne Borough	29
3204, 3207	1942–1946	Overbrook	210
2602	1940	Perry North	287
2614, 2615	1940–1948	Perry South	340
5220	1940	Pitcairn Borough	234
1404	1940	Point Breeze	323
1405	1943	Point Breeze North	119
605	1940	Polish Hill	62
5003	1948	Port Vue Borough	170
5140	1942	Rankin Borough	204
1410	1940	Regent Square	55
4281	1940	Reserve Township (1 of 2)	195
2016	1948	Ridgemont	25
4670	1943	Rosslyn Farms Borough	23

Table A.1—Continued

Census Tract	Median Year Structure Built	Neighborhood/Municipality	Number of Children Under 5 Years Old
4706	1944	Scott Township (1 of 4)	929
703, 05, 706, 708, 709	1941–1949	Shadyside	290
4240	1940	Sharpsburg	173
2018, 2022	1940–1946	Sheraden	432
409	1940	South Oakland	119
1609	1940	South Side Flats	142
1608	1940	South Side Slopes	222
2412	1940	Spring Garden	61
2620	1940	Spring Hill/City View	240
4171, 4172	1945–1948	Springdale Borough	167
1401	1940	Squirrel Hill North	265
1408, 1413, 1414	1940–1942	Squirrel Hill South	665
1018	1945	Stanton Heights	141
4621, 4626	1940–1947	Stowe Township	403
203	1940	Strip District	19
1411	1946	Swisshelm Park	55
5151, 5152, 5153, 5154, 5155	1940–1949	Swissvale Borough	553
4035	1940	Tarentum	287
511	1947	Terrace Village	209
5050	1940	Trafford Borough	165
5094	1941	Turtle Creek Borough	344
506	1940	Upper Hill	96
1011	1940	Upper Lawrenceville	181
5240	1942	Verona Borough	164
5010	1946	Versailles Borough	79
5060	1940	Wall Borough	30
4930	1940	West Elizabeth	34
2019	1940	West End	29

Table A.1—Continued

Census Tract	Median Year Structure Built	Neighborhood/Municipality	Number of Children Under 5 Years Old
4884	1949	West Mifflin Borough	1,187
402	1945	West Oakland	69
4301, 4302	1940–1946	West View Borough	446
4850	1943	Whitaker Borough	71
5604, 5605, 5606, 5610, 5611, 5612	1940–1946	Wilkinsburg Borough (6 of 8)	700
5080	1940	Wilmerding Borough	133
Total for all census tracts with median-age housing built before 1950			**31,823**

SOURCE: U.S. Census Bureau (2000a; 2000b).

Advisory Group Members

Ann Bertino
Board of Directors, Acting Executive Director,
Healthy Home Resources

Marc Cherna
Director,
Allegheny County Department of Human Services

Sylvia Choi
Pediatrician, Children's Hospital
Board of Directors,
Healthy Home Resources

Sharon Colaizzi
Director of Medical Management,
UPMC for You Health Plan

Bruce Dixon
Director,
Allegheny County Health Department

Ellen Dorsey
Program Officer, Environment,
The Heinz Endowments

Ann Jones Gerace
Interim Executive Director,
Healthy Home Resources

Bernard Goldstein
Dean, Graduate School of Public Health,
University of Pittsburgh

Bruce Good
Lead Program Chief,
Allegheny County Health Department

Peter Keim
Chief Medical Officer and Vice President,
Gateway Health Plan

Joseph McLaughlin
Administrator,
Pennsylvania Childhood Lead Poisoning Prevention Project (CLPPP),
Pennsylvania Department of Health

Sherlizia Murchison
Parent Leader,
Garfield Family Support Center

Robert Nelkin
Executive Director,
Governor's Cabinet for Children and Families

Joseph Sheridan
Medical Director, Three Rivers Administrative Services,
MedPlus+ Three Rivers Health Plan

Mike Tobin
ChemAdvisor, Inc.
Board of Directors,
Healthy Home Resources

Donald Yearsley
Director of Policy, Budgeting, and Planning,
Pennsylvania Department of Public Welfare,
Office of Medical Assistance Programs

A Comparison of Risk Factors for Lead Poisoning

Table C.1
A Comparison of Risk Factors for Lead Poisoning Across 12 Pennsylvania Counties and Rhode Island

County	Risk Factor						
	Total Population	Total Children Under 6 Years Old	Median Household Income in 1999	n Children Under 6 Years Old in Poverty	% Children Under 6 Years Old in Poverty	Median Age of Housing	% Built Before 1950
Allegheny	1,281,666	86,511	38,329	14,742	17.0	1952	45.5
Berks	373,638	27,834	44,714	4,095	14.7	1958	40.8
Chester	433,501	35,052	65,295	1,929	5.5	1973	20.5
Dauphin	251,798	18,131	41,507	3,035	16.7	1962	31.8
Erie	280,843	21,144	36,627	3,799	18.0	1957	39.4
Lackawanna	213,295	13,321	34,438	2,092	15.7	1942	56.6
Lancaster	470,658	39,798	45,507	4,900	12.3	1968	31.5
Lehigh	312,090	22,639	43,449	3,594	15.9	1960	36.2
Luzerne	319,250	19,455	33,771	3,589	18.4	1946	53.7
Montgomery	750,097	56,957	60,829	2,773	4.9	1963	28.8
Philadelphia	1,517,550	118,695	30,746	38,114	32.1	1945	58.4
York	381,751	28,302	45,268	2,692	9.5	1967	31.4
Rhode Island	**1,048,319**	**76,798**	**42,090**	**14,548**	**18.9**	**1958**	**39.2**

SOURCE: U.S. Census Bureau (2000a; 2000b).

References

AAP—see American Academy of Pediatrics.

American Academy of Child and Adolescent Psychiatry, "The Child with Autism, No. 11," *Facts for Families*, July 2004a. Online at http://www.aacap.org/publications/factsFam/autistic.htm (as of March 24, 2006).

———, "Children Who Can't Pay Attention/ADHD, No. 6," *Facts for Families*, July 2004b. Online at http://www.aacap.org/publications/factsFam/noattent.htm (as of March 24, 2006).

———, "The Depressed Child, No. 4," *Facts for Families*, July 2004c. Online at http://www.aacap.org/publications/factsFam/depressd.htm (as of March 24, 2006).

American Academy of Pediatrics, Committee on Environmental Health, "Screening for Elevated Blood Lead Levels," *Pediatrics,* Vol. 101, No. 6, June 1998, pp. 1072–1078.

American Academy of Pediatrics, Division of Health Policy Research, *Periodic Survey #28: Lead Screening Practices of Pediatricians*, Elk Grove Village, Ill., 1995. Online at http://www.aap.org/research/periodicsurvey/ps28exs.htm (as of March 24, 2006).

Baghurst, P. A., A. J. McMichael, N. R. Wigg, G. V. Vimpani, E. F. Robertson, R. J. Roberts, and S. L. Tong, "Environmental Exposure to Lead and Children's Intelligence at the Age of Seven Years: The Port Pirie Cohort Study," *New England Journal of Medicine*, Vol. 327, No. 18, October 29, 1992, pp. 1279–1284.

Beaman, C. A, "The Effect of Current Whole Blood Lead Levels on the Early Learning Abilities of Six-Year-Old Urban Children," unpublished dissertation, Detroit, Mich.: Wayne State University, 1998.

Bellinger D., H. Hu, L. Titlebaum, and H. L. Needleman, "Attentional Correlates of Dentin and Bone Lead Levels in Adolescents," *Archives of Environmental Health*, Vol. 49, No. 2, 1994, pp. 98–105.

Bellinger, D. C., and H. L. Needleman, "Intellectual Impairment and Blood Lead Levels," *New England Journal of Medicine*, Vol. 349, No. 5, July 31, 2003, p. 500.

Bellinger, D. C., K. M. Stiles, and H. L. Needleman, "Low-Level Lead Exposure, Intelligence and Academic Achievement: A Long-Term Follow-Up Study," *Pediatrics*, Vol. 90, No. 6, December 1, 1992, pp. 855–861.

Bhattacharya, A., R. Shukla, R. L. Bornschein, K. N. Dietricj, R. Keith, "Lead Effects on Postural Balance of Children," *Environmental Health Perspectives*, Vol. 89, 1990, pp. 35–42.

Canfield, R. L., C. R. Henderson, D. A. Cory-Slechta, C. Cox, T. A. Jusko, and B. P. Lanphear, "Intellectual Impairment in Children with Blood Lead Level Concentrations Below 10 µg per Deciliter," *New England Journal of Medicine*, Vol. 348, No. 16, April 17, 2003, pp. 1517–1526.

CDC—see Centers for Disease Control and Prevention.

Centers for Disease Control and Prevention, "Update: Blood Lead Levels—United States, 1991–1994," *Morbidity and Mortality Weekly Report*, Vol. 46, No. 7, February 21, 1997, pp. 141–146.

———, *Managing Elevated Blood Lead Levels Among Young Children: Recommendations from the Advisory Committee on Childhood Lead Poisoning Prevention*, Atlanta, Ga., March 2002. Online at http://www.cdc.gov/nceh/lead/CaseManagement/caseManage_main.htm (as of March 24, 2006).

———, "Blood Lead Levels—United States, 1999–2002," *Morbidity and Mortality Weekly Report*, Vol. 54, No. 20, May 27, 2005, pp. 513–527. Online at http://www.cdc.gov/mmwr/preview/mmwrhtml/mm5420a5.htm (as of March 24, 2006).

Centers for Disease Control and Prevention, National Center for Health Statistics, *Third National Health and Nutrition Examination Survey (NHANES), 1991–1994*, 1995.

———, National Center for Health Statistics, *National Immunization Survey*, Chicago, Ill.: National Opinion Research Center, 2003.

Centers for Disease Control and Prevention, National Center for Injury Prevention and Control, "Poisonings: Fact Sheet," August 5, 2004. Online at http://www.cdc.gov/ncipc/factsheets/Poisoning.htm (as of March 24, 2006).

Charney, E., B. Kessler, M. Farfel, and D. Jackson, "Childhood Lead Poisoning: A Controlled Trial of the Effect of Dust-Control Measures on Blood Lead Levels," *New England Journal of Medicine*, Vol. 309, No. 18, November 3, 1983, pp. 1089–1093.

Ellis, Mark R., and Kevin Y. Kane, "Lightening the Lead Load in Children," *American Family Physician*, Vol 62, No. 6, August 1, 2000. Online at http://www.aafp.org/afp/20000801/545.html (as of March 24, 2006).

Feingold, Mark, and Roberta L. Anderson, "Lessons and Tactics to Lead the Charge Against Lead Poisoning," *Contemporary Pediatrics*, Vol. 21, No. 4, April 1, 2004, pp. 49–68.

GAO—see U.S. General Accounting Office.

Halfon, Neal, Ericka Shulman, and Miles Hochstein, eds., "Brain Development in Early Childhood," *Building Community Systems for Young Children*, UCLA Center for Healthier Children, Families and Communities, August 2001. Online at http://www.healthychild.ucla.edu/Publications/Documents/halfon.health.dev.pdf (as of March 24, 2006).

HHS—see U.S. Department of Health and Human Services.

Hubal, Elaine A. Cohen, Linda S. Sheldon, Janet M. Burke, Thomas R. McCurdy, Maurice R. Berry, Marc L. Rigas, Valerie G. Zartarain, and Natalie C. G. Freeman, "Children's

Exposure Assessment: A Review of Factors Influencing Children's Exposure, and the Data Available to Characterize and Assess that Exposure," *Environmental Health Perspectives*, Vol. 108, No. 6, June 2000, pp. 475–486.

Kemper, Alex R., Lisa M. Cohn, Kathryn M. Fant, Kevin J. Dombkowski, and Sharon R. Hudson, "Follow-up Testing Among Children with Elevated Screening Blood Lead Levels," *Journal of the American Medical Association*, Vol. 293, No. 18, May 11, 2005, pp. 2232–2237.

Lane, Wendy G., and Alex R. Kemper, "American College of Preventive Medicine Practice Policy Statement: Screening for Elevated Blood Lead Levels in Children," *American Journal of Preventive Medicine*, Vol. 20, No. 1, January 2001, pp. 78–82.

McMichael, A. J., P. A. Baghurst, N. R. Wigg, G. V. Vimpani, E. F. Robertson, and R. J. Roberts, "Port Pirie Cohort Study: Environmental Exposure to Lead and Children's Abilities at the Age of Four Years," *New England Journal of Medicine*, Vol. 319, No. 8, August 25, 1988, pp. 468–475.

National Research Council, *Measuring Lead Exposure in Infants, Children, and Other Sensitive Populations*, Washington, D.C.: National Academy Press, 1993.

Needleman, H. L., "Childhood Lead Poisoning: The Promise and Abandonment of Primary Prevention," *American Journal of Public Health*, Vol. 88, No. 12, December 1, 1998, pp. 1871–1877.

Needleman, H. L., and D. C. Bellinger, "Type II Fallacies in the Study of Childhood Exposure to Lead at Low Dose: A Critical Quantitative Review," in M. A. Smith, L. D. Grant, and A. I. Sors, eds., *Lead Exposure and Child Development: An International Assessment*, Boston, Mass.: Kluwer Academic Publishers, 1989, pp. 293–304.

Needleman, H.L., and C. A. Gastonis, "Low-Level Lead Exposure and the IQ of Children: A Meta-Analysis of Modern Studies," *Journal of the American Medical Association*, Vol. 263, No. 5, February 2, 1990, pp. 673–678.

Needleman, H. L., C. Gunnoe, A. Leviton, R. Reed, H. Peresie, C. Maher, and P. Barrett, "Deficits in Psychologic and Classroom Performance of Children with Elevated Dentine Lead Levels," *New England Journal of Medicine*, Vol. 300, No. 13, March 29, 1979, pp. 689–695.

Needleman, H. L., A. Leviton, and D. Bellinger, "Lead-Associated Intellectual Deficit," *New England Journal of Medicine*, Vol. 306, No. 6, February 11, 1982, p. 367.

Needleman, H. L., J. A. Riess, M. J. Tobin, G. E. Biesecker, and J. B. Greenhouse, "Bone Lead Levels and Delinquent Behavior," *Journal of the American Medical Association*, Vol. 275, No. 5, February 7, 1996, pp. 363–369.

Owens-Stively, J., A. Spirito, M. Arrigan, and A. Alario, "Elevated Lead Levels and Sleep Disturbance in Young Children: Preliminary Findings," *Ambulatory Child Health*, Vol. 2, No. 3, 1997, pp. 221–229.

PA DOH—see Pennsylvania Department of Health.

PA DOI—see Pennsylvania Department of Insurance.

Pennsylvania Department of Health, *Lead Elimination Plan*, recommendations of the Lead Elimination Plan Workgroup, May 28, 2005. Online at http://www.dsf.health.state.pa.us/health/cwp/view.asp?A=179&Q=240544 (as of March 24, 2006).

Pennsylvania Department of Insurance, *The Health Insurance Status of Pennsylvanians: Statewide Survey Results*, Harrisburg, Pa., May 9, 2005.

Pennsylvania Partnerships for Children, *The State of the Child in Pennsylvania*, Harrisburg, Pa., 2004.

Pirkle, J. L., D. J. Brody, E. W. Gunter, R. A. Kramer, D. C. Paschal, K. M. Flegal, and T. D. Matte, "The Decline in Blood Lead Levels in the United States: The National Health and Nutrition Examination Surveys (NHANES)," *Journal of the American Medical Association*, Vol. 272, No. 4, July 27, 1994, pp. 284–291.

PPC—see Pennsylvania Partnerships for Children.

Public Health Service, *Toxicological Profile for Lead*, Atlanta, Ga.: U.S. Department of Health and Human Services, July 1999.

Rhoads, George G., Adrienne S. Ettinger, Clifford P. Weisel, Timothy J. Buckley, Karen Denard Goldman, John Adgate, and Paul J. Lioy, "The Effect of Dust Lead Control on Blood Lead in Toddlers: A Randomized Trial," *Pediatrics*, Vol. 103, No. 3, March 3, 1999, pp. 551–555.

Rhode Island Department of Health, Childhood Lead Poisoning Prevention Program, *Rhode Island Lead Screening Plan*, Providence, R.I., October 2000. Online at http://www.health.state.ri.us/lead/family/screeningplan.pdf (as of March 24, 2006).

Robinson, G. S., R. W. Keith, R. L. Bornschein, and D. A. Otto, "Effects of Environmental Lead Exposure on the Developing Auditory System as Indexed by the Brainstem Auditory Evoked Potential and Pure Tone Hearing Evaluations in Young Children," in S. E. Lindberg and T. C. Hutchinson, eds., *Heavy Metals in the Environment*, New Orleans, La.: CEP Consultants, Ltd., 1987, pp. 223–225.

Sargent, J. D., and M. A. Dalton, "Rethinking the Threshold for an Abnormal Capillary Blood Lead Screening Test," *Archives of Pediatrics and Adolescent Medicine*, Vol. 150, No. 10, October 1996, pp. 1084–1088.

Schlenker, T. L., C. J. Fritz, D. Mark, M. Layde, G. Linke, A. Murphy, and T. Matte, "Screening for Pediatric Lead Poisoning: Comparability of Simultaneously Drawn Capillary and Venous Blood Samples," *Journal of the American Medical Association*, Vol. 271, No. 17, May 4, 1994, pp. 1346–1348.

Schultz, Brad, David Pawel, and Amy Murphy, "A Retrospective Examination of In-Home Educational Visits to Reduce Childhood Lead Levels," *Environmental Research*, Vol. 80, No. 4, pp. 364–368.

Schwartz, J., and D. Otto, "Blood Lead, Hearing Thresholds, and Neurobehavioral Development in Children and Youth," *Archives of Environmental Health*, Vol. 42, No. 3, May/June 1987, pp. 153–160.

Sciarillo, W.G., G. Alexander, and K. P. Farrell, "Lead Exposure and Child Behavior," *American Journal of Public Health*, Vol. 82, No. 10, October 1992, pp. 1356–1360.

Stefanak, Matthew, Joe Diorio, and Larry Frisch, "Cost of Child Lead Poisoning to Taxpayers in Mahoning County, Ohio," *Public Health Reports*, Vol. 120, No. 3, May/June 2005, pp. 311–315.

University of Minnesota, School of Public Health, Maternal and Child Health Program, "Children's Special Vulnerability to Environmental Health Risks," *Healthy Generations*, Vol. 4, No. 3, February 2004, pp. 1–3. Online at http://www.epi.umn.edu/mch/resources/hg/hg_enviro.pdf (as of March 24, 2006).

U.S. Census Bureau, "Median Year Structure Built," Data Set SF3, Table H35, *2000 U.S. Census*, Washington, D.C., 2000a.

U.S. Census Bureau, "Sex by Age," Data Set SF1, Table P12, *2000 U.S. Census*, Washington, D.C., 2000b.

U.S. Department of Health and Human Services, *Strategic Plan for the Elimination of Childhood Lead Poisoning*, Washington, D.C., 1991.

———, "Objective 8-11: Eliminate Elevated Blood Lead Levels in Children," *Healthy People 2010*, 2000. Online at http://www.healthypeople.gov/document/html/objectives/08-11.htm (as of March 24, 2006).

———, "Best Practice Initiative: Improved Childhood Blood Lead Screening in Rhode Island," Rhode Island Department of Health, 2002. Online at http://phs.os.dhhs.gov/ophs/BestPractice/RI_bloodlead.htm (as of March 24, 2006).

U.S. General Accounting Office, *Medicaid: Elevated Blood Lead Levels in Children*, GAO/HEHS-98-78, Washington, D.C., February 1998. Online at http://www.gao.gov/archive/1998/he98078.pdf (as of March 24, 2006).

———, *Lead Poisoning: Federal Health Care Programs Are Not Effectively Reaching At-Risk Children*, report prepared for the Ranking Minority Member, Committee on Government Reform, House of Representatives, GAO/HEHS-99-18, Washington, D.C., January 1999. Online at http://www.gao.gov/archive/1999/he99018.pdf (as of March 24, 2006).

Vivier, Patrick M., Joseph W. Hogan, Peter Simon, Tricia Leddy, Lynne M. Dansereau, and Anthony J. Alario, "A Statewide Assessment of Lead Screening Histories of Preschool Children Enrolled in a Medicaid Managed Care Program," *Pediatrics*, Vol. 108, No. 2, August 2001, p. e29.